Love, Jesus, Sex

Experiences & Lessons Learned

by Shannon Nicole Taylor

09/08/2018

From: Shannon Taylor

TO: Momma D

Copyright © 2017 by Shannon Taylor

All rights reserved. This book or any portion thereof may not be reproduced or used in any manner whatsoever without the express written permission of the author except for the use of brief quotations in a book review.

Unless otherwise noted, Scripture quotations are from the HOLY BIBLE, NEW INTERNATIONAL VERSION®. Copyright 1973, 1978, 1984 by International Bible Society. Used by permission. All rights reserved.

Scripture quotations marked AMP are from the Amplified Bible. Copyright 2015 by The Lockman Foundation, La Habra, CA 90631. All rights reserved. Used by permission.

Scripture quotations noted NKJV are from THE NEW KING JAMES VERSION. Copyright 1979, 1980, 1982, 1990, 1994, Thomas Nelson, Inc., Publishers.

Scripture quotations noted NLT are from the *Holy Bible,* NEW LIVING TRANSLATION, copyright 1996. Used by permission. All rights reserved.

Scripture quotations marked THE MESSAGE are from *The Message: The Bible in Contemporary English,* copyright 1993, 1994, 1995, 1996, 2000, 2001, 2002. Used by permission of NavPress Publishing Group.

First Printing, 2017 Printed in the United States of America

Library of Congress Cataloging-in-Publication Data:
An application to register this book for cataloging has been submitted to the Library of Congress.
International Standard Book Number:
ISBN-13:978-1544098753
ISBN-10:1544098758

10 9 8 7 6 5 4 3 2 1

This book is dedicated to my husband Richard, daughters Maya and Ava and my son Caleb. Thank you for loving me unconditionally! Richard, thank you for putting up with me through this process. God knows it's been a journey! To everyone who's ever prayed for me, blessed me financially, counseled me, listened to me, allowed me to speak into their lives, allowed me to cry it out, talk it out, scream it out, thank you and may God bless you abundantly!

-Shannon N. Taylor

TABLE OF CONTENTS

INTRODUCTION	1
MY STORY	3
IN THE BEGINNING…	6
THE GREAT SHAKE DOWN!	12
LOVE WITHOUT LIMITS	19
BEFORE YOU SAY, "I DO" …	24
JUST BE!	29
POWERFUL LOVE	33
BOUNDARIES	36
WHO DO YOU THINK YOU ARE?	39
ATTRACTING LOVE	42
RE-VIEW YOUR BODY	46
DARE TO BE DIFFERENT!	49
WHO'S YOUR HUBBY?	52
DROP YOUR BAGS!	55

THE RIB	58
HE DOES THAT FOR ME?	63
TRUST ME!	66
TRUSTING GOD'S PLAN FOR YOUR LIFE	70
THE IMPORTANCE OF BEING IN HIS PRESENCE DAILY	74
GOD'S PERFECT TIMING	79
KEEP YOUR EYES ON THE PRIZE	81
CHOSEN!	84
ALWAYS COME BACK TO THIS	87
WHAT'S REALLY IMPORTANT TO GOD?	91
PRECIOUS WOMAN OF GOD	97
CHANGE	100
CRUTCH	103
5 THINGS TO THINK ABOUT BEFORE YOU HAVE SEX	107
OVERCOMING THE DESIRE TO FORNICATE	110
CLOUDY VISION	115

TRUTH & LIES	118
FACING TRUTH	123
TEMPTATION IS A BEAST!	126
SCRIPTURES FOR WHEN YOU'RE BEING TEMPTED	129
HOW TO SAY NO	132
TRIGGERS	135
SELF-CONTROL	140
CRAVINGS	143
PLEASING SELF	145
HOW WILL I KNOW?	148
NOTHING NEW UNDER THE SUN!	151
REWARD?	154
GIVING UP RIGHTS	157
WHAT DID YOU DO?	164
THE LONG ARM OF DISOBEDIENCE & DECEPTION	167
WHAT I WISH I'D KNOWN ABOUT SEX BEFORE I GOT MARRIED	172

INTRODUCTION

My Dearest Sister,

I thank you so much for purchasing this book. You could have chosen any other book in this whole wide world, but you chose mine, and I want you to know that you are greatly appreciated!

There are a few things I want you to know about this book. You are holding a piece of my heart. This is not your normal, conventional book. It's not necessarily in a chronological or story format. It's not really a devotional unless you want it to be. This book is filled with lessons, some hard and painful, some sweet. Each section, each page gives a different picture or aspect of who I am and what I and so many others have gone or is going through. What you're reading are the stories of my life and those I've been privileged to do life with.

My goal, hope, wish for this book is to impart wisdom, sister to sister, in the areas of love, our relationship with Jesus and sex, that will help you or someone you know. It is my prayer that you will learn from my mistakes, my lessons, my teachings my rebukes.

You might even find that some of the information in each section is redundant. This is not my doing, but Holy Spirit's. I see it as His way of reminding us to, in all things, keep our eyes on Him! It is my prayer that this book will point you to the only ONE who will EVER fully satisfy the deepest voids in your heart, soul, and spirit. The only ONE who will ever truly understand you and what you're going through. The true LOVER of your soul, our Lord and Savior Jesus Christ.

May God bless you abundantly,

Shannon

1 Corinthians 6:12-20 MSG

12 Just because something is technically legal doesn't mean that it's spiritually appropriate. If I went around doing whatever I thought I could get by with, I'd be a slave to my whims.

13 You know the old saying, "First you eat to live, and then you live to eat"? Well, it may be true that the body is only a temporary thing, but that's no excuse for stuffing your body with food, or indulging it with sex. Since the Master honors you with a body, honor him with your body!

14-15 God honored the Master's body by raising it from the grave. He'll treat yours with the same resurrection power. Until that time, remember that your bodies are created with the same dignity as the Master's body. You wouldn't take the Master's body off to a whorehouse, would you? I should hope not.

16-20 There's more to sex than mere skin on skin. Sex is as much spiritual mystery as physical fact. As written in Scripture, "The two become one." Since we want to become spiritually one with the Master, we must not pursue the kind of sex that avoids commitment and intimacy, leaving us lonelier than ever—the kind of sex that can never "become one." There is a sense in which sexual sins are different from all others. In sexual sin we violate the sacredness of our own bodies, these bodies that were made for God-given and God-modeled love, for "becoming one" with another. Or didn't you realize that your body is a sacred place, the place of the Holy Spirit? Don't you see that you can't live however you please, squandering what God paid such a high price for? The physical part of you is not some piece of property belonging to the spiritual part of you. God owns the whole works. So, let people see God in and through your body.

My Story

On a fake brown leather sofa of his girlfriend's apartment, I had my first sexual experience. I was 14 years old, and he was 22. I can't remember if it was during the summer or after school one day but this day had been in the works as we'd had the discussion mapping out the details. He told me how I wouldn't have to worry or be scared because he wouldn't tell anyone. The day came, and I think I'd changed into something loose and I think I'd removed my panties. I went to the apartment after his girlfriend had left, and in a matter of minutes, I'd given away two very precious gifts; my virginity and innocence. No love, no protection, just sex. The whole experience was extremely painful and scary. I felt violated, open, and it all just felt wrong! Definitely not what you see in the movies and on TV. I didn't know what I was doing, and I fully trusted him because he was older, cute, and he "liked" me. He'd charmed and persuaded me saying he would be gentle and most importantly, he wouldn't tell anyone. To make matters worse, he and his girlfriend knew my mom, and they lived across the hall from me.

I went home afterward and the only one I told at the time was my sister. The second time was at a friend's house with the same guy, still painful but somehow, I didn't feel guilt or shame. I felt grown up, cool, and wanted, or so I thought. After all, sex was the thing to do. I didn't know anything different, wasn't taught otherwise. By the time my mom decided to try to teach me anything about sex, I'd already gone to get birth control pills, which she'd found hidden in a brown paper bag behind my bed.

- After all this, I'd declared I wouldn't have sex again until I was 17 years old! Yeah, I know, I still hadn't learned anything! Well, at 16, I had sex again with a guy who claimed to love me but didn't really because he tried and succeeded in having sex with my cousin. This behavior of looking for love and giving myself away continued in college as well. One heartbreak after another.

- I say all this to point out one simple but profound fact, I was never taught the truth about sex. I was never taught that sex is a gift from God given to married couples – male and female – as a means of expression of their love for one another! Also, sex is a representation of the most intimate relationship we are to have with God. God never intended for me or any of us to give ourselves away so freely and to be hurt and broken repeatedly. Sex is to be reserved for the marriage bed. We are to be pure until we are married.

- When you have sex with someone, you become one with them, body, soul, and spirit. I wish someone had told me to wait, to give my body to my husband! If I'd known the truth about sex, about God, I wouldn't have given myself away so freely and easily looking for love, wanting to feel needed, accepted and loved. All that was already there waiting for me through the unconditional love of God!

- If I'd known about the magnificent love of God, I could have avoided so many heartaches, heartbreaks, emotional scars, and disappointments. No one can or will ever love us the way God does and even though I've made so many mistakes, what Satan meant for bad, destruction and to end my life, my Father in Heaven has turned it around for my good!

So, if you have had sex, you can always stop and receive God's forgiveness and redemption, and walk in His love and freedom. If you haven't had sex yet, please, WAIT!

- God put this on my heart, to spread His truth about this wonderful gift that He has given us and if I can help even one person, then my purpose has been fulfilled.

~Thoughts~

In The Beginning...

As a Christian now, I look back and wish that all the things I know now, I could go back and tell the young Shannon everything that I've learned. I would tell her to turn left here, not right, don't go there with this person and don't have sex at all until you're married! Had I known God, I would have had the direction I needed. But I have come to know that God is faithful and that no matter how bad, or painful things are in life, miraculously He can and will turn them around for our good and that sometimes through our pain our purpose will come. (Romans 8:28 NLT – And we know that God causes everything to work together for the good of those who love God and are called according to his purpose for them)

I grew up in a single-parent home with my mom and sister. My mom was a sweetheart, very loving and funny but she was controlled by her addiction to drugs and alcohol. Her addictions eventually killed her. While her addictions made my and my sister's life very painful, I still loved my mom unconditionally, but I can't help but wonder how different our lives would have been if she had a deep relationship with Jesus Christ?

I've noticed that not much has changed since my younger days except the fact that people are a heck of a lot bolder and daring it seems! When you are young, fitting in and being accepted is the ultimate goal. Unfortunately, I never reached that goal. I was definitely an outsider! I walked funny, or what's called knock-kneed, I was shy, never wore the coolest clothes or shoes, and I just didn't fit with the "in" crowd. Now, I'm very grateful that I didn't fit in, but in junior high and high school, oh it mattered, tremendously. On top of being teased about my appearance, I was teased about my family, my mom in particular. One of her drug suppliers went to my high school, and he wasn't interested in keeping my mom's habit and the fact that my mom owed him money a secret. He wanted his money, and he made a point to share this information with me at school in the hallway in everyone's earshot! Oh, the horror of it all! The teasing was incessant and unbearable. "Your mom is a crack head!" "Look at your shoes and clothes!" "Why do you walk that way?" These words stung like no other. I was without a doubt, miserable! But as I got older and started attracting attention from the opposite sex, these things didn't seem to bother me as much. After all, if boys were paying attention to me then maybe there was hope for me, right? I figured if the boys like me then I must be ok. My escape from the pains of my life came from the acceptance and attention I received from boys especially the older ones. Oh, that was just awesome to me! Older boys thought I was cute and cool! In a young teenage girl's mind, you just couldn't beat that!

Not only did my mom have the drug and alcohol problems, but she also had all the accompanying health problems that come along with it. We received public assistance at the beginning of every month, and if she didn't get to the grocery store by the third day of the month we were screwed! The money would be blown on drugs and alcohol. No food, no clean clothes, nothing. There were times when my sister and I had to wash our clothes by hand and let them dry overnight in the utility closet. This method sucked in the summer, worked ok in the winter. Some days we would go to school with damp, smoke smelly clothes. So, any distraction I could get from my present circumstances were welcomed with open arms!

I learned the hard way about sex, and I found out things on my own and from peers who didn't know any more than I did. I guess my mom figured I was smart and that I'd figure things out on my own. She didn't work full time, and the only jobs she had as a housekeeper for hotels were only part-time when she was able to keep a job. Seems she only kept a job long enough to get one paycheck to blow on a good time. It wasn't until she found my birth control pills that she decided to ask if I was having sex. Of course, I lied and said the pills belonged to someone else. Somehow, she'd gotten pamphlets with pictures of all the sexually transmitted diseases and gave them to me. I can't remember much of what she told me after that because sex had already been introduced to me. I'd already lost my virginity to the 22-year-old. Surely older guys knew what they were doing, right? I could trust him, right? The attention from the 22-year-old him was a welcomed distraction from the dysfunction in my day to day life. Everyone liked him, but he liked me. That fateful day on the fake, brown leather couch produced more pain, bad circumstances, and consequences than I could ever imagine and they led to more bad choices.

No one else around me was waiting for sex. The only thing they were waiting for was the right opportunity to do so! I wasn't told how you sin against your own body and that each time you have sex with someone, you give yourself away and "become one" repeatedly, your soul tied to someone who could care less about you or your feelings. You do NOT have to give yourself away! You do NOT have to prove yourself to anyone! Do NOT be pressured into doing something that will change your life sexually, mentally, emotionally, and most of all, spiritually. This is NOT God's plan for you! He loves you too much and wants to protect you. The precepts that are in the Bible are boundaries, not restrictions to keep you from living life and having fun.

God gave us gifts: sex, virginity, and our body. However, there are consequences for abusing the gifts given to us. Look around, unwanted pregnancies, abortions, diseases, teen pregnancy, dysfunctional families, emotional, spiritual, and physical damage, wrong decisions, etc. The list goes on. God knew what He was doing when He reserved sex for marriage. He wanted to prevent this all from happening. He meant for us to experience life as Adam and Eve did before the fall. Yes, there are reasons He says to wait. I wish I had. I wish that I'd shared all these gifts with my husband first. I hope my story, experiences, and lessons learned will make you think long and hard about having sex before marriage and living your life without God. And if you are or have had sex outside of marriage I pray that you stop and wait until marriage to experience sex the way God intended: without shame, guilt, or inhibitions. I pray that you will treasure yourself and most of all begin or deepen your relationship with God. He's always there, waiting and watching, wanting to be in a relationship with us. Waiting for us to receive the wonderful gift of salvation. But when we don't choose Him, His presence or Lordship in our lives, then He's absent from our choices and decisions. When we say no to God, it's as if we're saying, "I got this and I don't need your help!" "I know what I need and want and what's best for me"! I have come to know that we don't know what's best! We don't know anything! There are lasting consequences of choices and decisions of saying no to God. It's not easy, this I know for a fact. Choosing God is the greatest decision I've ever made, and now I have the abundant life that He promised me in His Word, and you can too!

~Thoughts~

The Great Shake Down!

I met my husband in 2001 in college, although when I met him, I had no clue he would be my husband, none of that love at first sight stuff. He was just this cute dude I would see on campus who also had a very nice butt! Yes, there was lust, and it didn't help that he had muscles in all the right places and gorgeous eyes! So, each time I saw him, it was a treat for my eyes! Well, it just so happens, that I ended up having a class with Mr. Fine and he was even in my group for our class group project. I never knew his name until the class, and for the first three classes, he was missing in action. When he decided to show up for class that's when I could put a name with the muscles and cute behind of Mr. Fine. His name was Richard, Rich for short. I paid no attention to him at first because he looked so young, but he wouldn't have it that way, he made sure that I knew who he was! The semester moves along, and he and I got closer, and he turned out to not only be cute but very smart, intelligent, and ambitious. He had his whole life mapped out (or so he thought)! I thought that was awesome coming from someone so young, then I find he's only 2 years younger than me, but he looked so young! Anyway, moving further through time, we got to know each other better and began dating. In the process, he began having issues with his roommate who eventually bailed on him and left him with the full responsibility of the apartment they shared. Things got rough, and he had to move out and had nowhere to go, so he moved in with me. Yeah, I know……. Ok, here's where things start to go crazy...

Now, before I met Rich, God had been calling me to come back to him, but I didn't want to "give up" my "freedom". So, I was occasionally going to church. One day when I was volunteering at church, I learned that living together with someone of the opposite sex before marriage was wrong, that this was called "shacking up". Whoa, wait a minute you mean, everyone I grew up around that's been "shacking up" is wrong and that's not the way that God meant for things to be?! But I have this cute boyfriend who had "nowhere else to go" who now lives with me! Oh no, what do we do? As God would have it, Rich and I were able to forge a friendship with this married couple at our church who basically broke things down for us. We had a choice to make: boyfriend moves out, or we get married! Say huh? Marriage was not on the agenda. We were trying to graduate from college first and we never even talked about marriage before. We sat on this information and sat, and sat and sat until "The Great Shake Down" happened.

Let me preface this. When you surrender your life to Christ, He loves you too much to let you wallow in your sin and if you don't do anything about it, He will, and that's just what He did. "The Great Shakedown" begins. First, Rich wrecked his car, he was fine, but the car wasn't and being a broke college student that meant no new car for a while. During this, I was going through pure heck in the job I had, so I decided to quit just knowing I would get another in no time, but 9/11 happened, and the job didn't come as fast as I thought it would. After my job ordeal, my car broke down, and we couldn't afford to get it fixed nor could I afford to keep up the payments so, my car was repossessed. Rich lost his job but found another, but it wasn't enough to carry us and the apartment, so we were evicted. Thankfully, I had a friend that I could move in with, so I put my things in storage and moved in with her and Rich went to room with some guy he knew from college. Well, the arrangement with Rich lasted a week or two, and then he moved in with my friend and me. Sad to say, we still didn't get the hints that were being thrown at us. So, we continued going to church, and God continued making his statement. He *humbled* us! We were in an area that wasn't the most pleasant, we had no cars, so it was public transportation for us, I had to work at a restaurant which was the absolute last thing I wanted to do, and it didn't pay a lot of money and we were in the very last semesters of college before graduation, so the stress was almost unbearable! In the midst of this, we slipped and had sex. Even though we knew the truth now, it was still hard to fight the temptation because we still lived together and slept in the same bed. Yes, we were asking for it! After much struggle and hustling to finish school and work stressful jobs, Rich and I were hurt, defeated, and exhausted. Everything was so difficult! Just getting to school and work was a feat! We waved the white flag and prayed, God, if it's your will for us to be together and get married, then show us what to do, make a way for us. We had no money, so if this was going to happen, God had to help us with this!

After we had prayed, we stepped out in faith and went to see my friend who worked at a jewellery store, we told him our situation, and to our surprise, he was able to get us an awesome deal and use his discount! Rich and I looked at each other and thought ok, hmm this went very well. So, after we picked out our rings, we went on to finish school. Rich graduated before me and a few months after, I graduated. Then on November 8, 2003, he proposed! He was no longer boyfriend, but now fiancé! I was so shocked, and to this day, I still don't remember what he said when he proposed, and neither does he. Sad, right? After this, I graduated from college, and we went about the business of getting married. My plan was to purchase a little party dress, nothing extravagant because broke college students can't afford the extravagant. God had other plans! My friend, Rich and I went to this little dress shop, and Ms. Charlotte greeted us, and we told her we were getting married, and I just needed a little party dress nothing extravagant because we had no money. Ms. Charlotte, says no, no, you're getting a wedding dress! Rich and I looked at each other and just followed.

Well to sum it all up, I got a beautiful wedding dress, veil, and all adjustments for a total of $383.00! Again, God made a way! We met with our pastor, <u>once</u> (um, another story for another day, sheesh!!) and he proceeds to tell us that since we were living together and were not married, we needed to get married ASAP oh, and stop having sex! He never explained why or the spiritual consequences, just stop having sex. No advice, no nothing. So, we set a date for February 6, 2004. It all worked out because we got our taxes done early! Praise God! We gave the pastor a $100 "love offering", had close friends there which totalled 15 people at our wedding (no family there at all). My friend and the lady in the floral department from Kroger made my bouquet, another friend got us a ridiculous discount on a Jacuzzi suite for our honeymoon. I walked myself down the aisle and Rich's best friend was the ring bearer, and my bestie was my maid of honor, and on February 6, 2004, we became Mr. & Mrs. Richard W. Taylor II!

We are still married, and the road hasn't been easy, but we know that God is in our marriage and that's also another lesson for another day. Now, why do I tell you all this? Some people argue that living together before you get married is not a sin because it's not in the Bible and it's not, but God is a God of order, and there's a reason for not living together before marriage. When you do this, you set yourself up for failure, pain, and destruction. It's only by the grace of God that I didn't get pregnant while we were playing house and that we were both able to graduate from college but it did cause problems in our marriage (more on this later) not only this but, we still had to deal with the repercussions of us having sex with each other before we were married. Sex is spiritual, so you better believe that there will be some spiritual warfare going on! My other point is you can't say that you're a child of God and still blatantly sin and decide you're going to do things your way. With God, it doesn't work this way, either you belong to Him, or you don't, and if you do, He's going to make sure that you do things the way that He says to keep you from hurting yourself and bringing everything but glory to His name. Lastly, is that if you decide to commit your way to Him, He will show up and show you favor and make things happen for you that you wouldn't believe! So, if you're shacking up right now, I encourage you to make some decisions so that you won't have to endure "The Great Shakedown!" If you're not ready for marriage, pray for God to make other living arrangements and go where He sends you and if you are ready, then *get premarital counselling* and take heed to all you're being taught. DO NOT set a wedding date until after counselling because you never know what will come up and out during counselling. Trust me I've seen the horror of a marriage happening even though they were told that they were not ready! They are paying dearly for it! Take your time and do things in order the way God intended. Marriage is not something to rush into and trying to practice it before you say, "I do" is just asking for trouble! Take your time and pray. Have accountability partners, stay pure and trust God!

~Thoughts~

LOVE

Jeremiah 31:3 NKJ
The Lord has appeared of old to me, saying: "Yes, I have loved you with an everlasting love; Therefore, with loving kindness I have drawn you.

Love without Limits

What do you think of when you hear the words "unconditional love"? Do you think of the love parents have for their children or the love God has for us? I think of both, but mainly the love God has for us, His daughters. I can never seem to wrap my mind around the unconditional love that God has for His children. I try, in my little finite mind, to put it into terms that I can understand, but it's humanly impossible. I believe that is because we must work at loving others unconditionally; it doesn't come naturally.

We can try to love the people in our lives unconditionally on our own, but we may miss a few important components that are involved in loving someone this way. Patience, forgiveness, mercy, and grace are all required. Loving our spouses and our family members requires these things. But with God's mercy and grace, we can extend unconditional love to others.

He leads by example. *"For God loved the world so much that he gave his one and only Son so that everyone who believes in him will not perish but have eternal life"* **(John 3:16 NLT).** He's the master at loving unconditionally. But what is so beautiful about unconditional love, you may ask? The beauty in it is that God is love; He makes it beautiful!

Unconditional love is defined as a profoundly tender, passionate affection for another person, without conditions or limitations. God is passionate about His love for us. He expresses His love in His Word. We as women need to know that we are loved. It's part of our makeup. Because we like the sappy love notes and letters, I look at God's Word as His love letter to us. In His love, there is no judgment, no fear, and no favoritism and we don't have to work for it. To Him, love is important; it's not taken lightly and thrown around at will. When He says He loves us, He means it!

Such love has no fear because perfect love expels all fear. If we are afraid, it is for fear of punishment, and this shows that we have not fully experienced his perfect love. ***1 John 4:18 (NLT)***

*The Lord appeared to us in the past, saying: "I have loved you with an everlasting love; I have drawn you with loving-kindness.*** Jeremiah 31:3 (NIV 84)***

Love Is the Greatest. If I could speak all the languages of earth and of angels but didn't love others, I would only be a noisy gong or a clanging cymbal. If I had the gift of prophecy, and if I understood all of God's secret plans and possessed all knowledge, and if I had such faith that I could move mountains, but didn't love others, I would be nothing. If I gave everything I have to the poor and even sacrificed my body, I could boast about it; but if I didn't love others, I would have gained nothing. Love is patient and kind. Love is not jealous or boastful or proud or rude. It does not demand its own way. It is not irritable, and it keeps no record of being wronged. It does not rejoice about injustice but rejoices whenever the truth wins out. Love never gives up, never loses faith, is always hopeful, and endures through every circumstance. Prophecy and speaking in unknown languages and special knowledge will become useless. But love will last forever! Now our knowledge is partial and incomplete, and even the gift of prophecy reveals only part of the whole picture! But when the time of perfection comes, these partial things will become useless. When I was a child, I spoke and thought and reasoned as a child. But when I grew up, I put away childish things. Now we see things imperfectly, like puzzling reflections in a mirror, but then we will see everything with perfect clarity. All that I know now is partial and incomplete, but then I will know everything completely, just as God now knows me completely. Three things will last forever—faith, hope, and love—and the greatest of these is love.
1 Corinthians 13:1-13 (NLT)

His Word shows us that His love, unlike ours, isn't based on what we have, how much we have, how we look, how we dress, or where we live. His love is truly unconditional, and it doesn't change. The fact is, there is nothing we can do to make Him not love us. We are His daughters, and He knows our hurts, struggles, mistakes, and hang-ups. He is just waiting for us to let Him love us through it all and despite it all.

God doesn't require us to get ourselves together first to experience His unconditional love. He wants us to find comfort in knowing we can come to Him dirty, filthy, and weighed down; then we can be washed, unburdened, and made whole. *"... for His yoke is easy to bear, and the burden He gives us is light"* **(Matthew 11:30 NLT)**. In Him, we are made beautiful, by Love Himself.

"To all who mourn in Israel, he will give a crown of beauty for ashes, a joyous blessing instead of mourning, festive praise instead of despair. In their righteousness, they will be like great oaks that the Lord has planted for his own glory" **(Isaiah 61:3 NLT)**.

~Thoughts~

Before you say, "I do" ...

I am not nor do I claim to be a marriage expert, but I can speak from my experiences. I have been married for some years, and it has been one of the most amazing, beautifully challenging rides of my life! There's been some good, some bad and some ugly! I've come to find that marriage is truly what you make it. You must make up your mind that you're going to love this person no matter what.

My hubby and I went into marriage totally unprepared. We knew we loved each other, but we knew absolutely nothing about marriage! **Even more so, we knew nothing about how marriage was supposed to look according to God's Word.** We had one hour of premarital counseling, and that was it. Because we only had one hour of counselling, we learned about marriage through many trials and many errors. Granted, it has made us stronger, and now we're able to pass some wisdom and knowledge on to others, the first seven years of our marriage was hard and sometimes painful. Honestly, I feel the reason a lot of marriages don't last is because the couples go in unprepared. The time isn't taken in the "getting to know you phase" to talk about the things that are truly important in marriage.

Now, I can only speak from a woman's point of view, my point of view. I want my single ladies who are constantly praying for a hubby to make sure YOU'RE ready for marriage (remember, God brought Eve to Adam Genesis 2:22). In marriage, a woman is to respect and love her hubby no matter what…are you ready for this? Whether you feel like it or not. Love is a choice and not always an easy one as well as respect. A wife is also expected to be submissive, but some women have issues with being submissive. It's not like the stigma that's out there. Submission is not the man telling you what to do, and you must do it, submission is respecting your husband as head of household and trusting that whatever decisions he makes, he's consulted with God first and have chosen what's best for you and your family. Now, if He hasn't consulted with God, take heart, the end results fall on him, not you. So, here's a concise list of things to think of, talk about with your potential hubby and take care of before you say, "I do":

1. Does he respect you?
2. Do you respect him?
3. Do you trust him with your life, to guide and direct you (and your family)?
4. How does he feel about being head of household, better yet, does he even know what it means?
5. Does he love Jesus more than he loves you? (THIS IS CRITICAL IN THE WAY THAT HE WILL LOVE AND TREAT YOU!)
6. How does he handle money?
7. Who is in his circle of friends? Who influences him?
8. How does he feel about having children? What are his views on discipline?
9. Make sure you both understand the role of a husband and wife!
10. Please make sure to talk about how the money will be handled in your marriage. If not, it can tear your marriage apart!
11. **DO NOT HAVE SEX UNTIL YOU SAY I DO! (If you are having sex, STOP!**

ON A PERSONAL NOTE:

12. Where are you in your walk with God? Are you getting married for the right reasons? (NOTE: YOUR SPOUSE IS NOT SUPPOSED TO AND CANNOT FULFILL ALL YOUR NEEDS! THERE ARE NEEDS THAT YOUR SPOUSE IS TO FILL AND THERE ARE NEEDS THAT ONLY GOD CAN FILL!)
13. Are you happy with who you are?
14. What's most important to you now, career or family? Not saying that you can't have both, but sometimes when you get married and have kids, things can and will change. How flexible are you?
15. Know what your needs and desires are and think of the ones that are most important to you. If affection is an absolute must-have for you, then if the guy you're with is not giving you that, don't think that just because you get married, he's going to automatically become affectionate. Marriage is not a magic wand!
16. Do you know what his needs and desires are and do you feel that you can meet them?

I repeat, I am not and don't claim to be a marriage expert, all I can tell you is what I've experienced and have seen. If you feel you've found your mate, then please go through premarital counselling, and don't live together while going through the process. Do things God's way, in His order, and He will tell you all you need to know and what to do. Trust God, you will need Him when you get married! Satan hates marriage because it is blessed by God (see Genesis 5:1-2) so he will try all he can to separate you, make you fight, argue, use the things you once thought were cute to annoy you among other underhanded tricks. My point is: don't underestimate Satan!

Scriptural References:
Genesis 2:18
Genesis 2:22-24
Psalm 15:4
Song of Songs (Song of Solomon)
1 Corinthians 6:12-20
1 Corinthians 7
Ephesians 5:22-33
Philippians 2:3
Colossians 3:18-19
Titus 2:4-5
Hebrews 13:4
1 Peter 3:1-7

~Thoughts~

Just Be!

ESTHER 2:15B (MSG) ESTHER, JUST AS SHE WAS, WON THE ADMIRATION OF EVERYONE WHO SAW HER.

The Lord had me study Esther, and at first, I wasn't sure why, but as I started reading through the first two chapters, I began to see what He was getting at.

I'd begun the most awesome opportunity of being the purity program coordinator at my church, and I'm still amazed at how all this came about but of course with this opportunity came many questions from myself of whether I felt that I could really do this. Was I ready? Would the women like me or receive me and what I had to say? Would I freeze up and forget everything I'd learned? So, God, being the amazing Father that He is, took heed of my questions, doubts, insecurities and lack of confidence and nervousness and led me to an example that would help me through this. I thought at first that I had to change who I was, but I learned that just by being Shannon, God could work wonders!

As I began reading through the first two chapters of Esther, especially in chapter two, it's mentioned 3 times that Esther had found favor from those around her (Esther 2:9, 15, 17). I'm looking at these verses, and I read them in different translations. I noticed that the scriptures don't really say how she obtained favor. She didn't change anything to obtain favor from Hagai, the eunuch in charge of the women, but somehow Esther pleased him and obtained his favor, and he immediately gave her the beauty treatments and preparations needed before she was to go in to the king (2:9). Also, when it was time for her to go in to the king, she asked Hagai for advice on what to take, and she didn't act as if she knew it all or that she had it all together. From this, I saw humility and maybe even a little nervousness and insecurity.

By Esther showing this side of herself, it says that she obtained favor in the sight of all who saw her (2:15). Then, once she's in with the king, it says that the king loved Esther more than all the other women and she obtained grace <u>and</u> favor in his sight, more than all the other virgins! It doesn't say that she did something amazing or fascinating, she was just Esther. So, by Esther being Esther, and not trying to be whom she thought she was supposed to be or who someone else thought she was supposed to be, she obtained favor! The book of Esther never mentions God, but you can see His hand in all that happened in this book. He was behind the scenes orchestrating events for His purposes. He didn't ask Esther for directions or help, she was just a willing vessel! In her willingness to just be, God used her, provided all she needed by His amazing grace and favor, and all she had to do was just be Esther!

So, my answer to my nervousness, insecurity, and thinking I had to be someone else was to just be Shannon! All that I am, He created, and that's what He wants me to be! He chose me just as I am to do what He has called me to be and do. I was created for this, no changes to be someone else are needed. Yes, I've had to grow in some areas, which comes with the territory of leading others, but I didn't have to and don't have to pretend to be someone I'm not. I can be my happy, joyful, silly yet firm self, and still be used by God in a mighty way! Why should I try to hide the amazing joy that I have? God has seen me through some painful situations and has turned them around for His purposes and my good. It's insulting to try to change what He's done as if what He's done isn't enough! To top it all off, my Father knows I learn things by watching, I'm a visual learner. I asked Him, for example, how to be confident but humble in what He has me doing because more

than anything, humility is very important to me and especially to God. Hello, pride is what got Satan kicked out of heaven!
One day I was sitting on the sofa watching the *Cosby Show* with my daughters, and I heard Holy Spirit say, "Clair Huxtable" and I said, what about her? He said, "She's confident but humble." So, I watched her and her actions, and that gave me peace and the visual example I needed!

All of this to say to you, my dear sisters, just be! Just be who God created you to be. If there are things you need to change that you know are contrary to His word, then pray and ask Him to help you to change them, but don't go and try to change who you are to please others, which is a sin by the way, because we're here to please God and not man (Galatians 1:10). Don't try to change to get attention from men, or fake your way to a promotion, or to try to make others accept you, you are already enough for whatever purpose God created you for. You are enough for your future hubby. God will bring you to him in due time (Genesis 2:22). Change what God tells you to change that's contrary to Him but otherwise just be you. You are fearfully and wonderfully made by the Almighty (Psalm 139). Yes, you are to take care of His temple, your body, but make sure you're doing it for the right reasons, for your health and to glorify Him, and not because you want attention from the opposite sex. Are you dressing your temple in a way that pleases and glorifies God or in a way that will cause your brother to stumble, lust and eventually fall? You don't have to and shouldn't follow all the trends of this world for attention or to fill whatever you feel that's missing from your life. Just be and allow God to fill all that's missing in your life. You are enough! Say it: I AM ENOUGH!

~Thoughts~

Powerful Love ♡

Love can be deep and intense. It can cause you to do things that you don't understand and things that you wouldn't normally do. Love can feed you, encourage you, keep you moving, and help you to be all that you want, need, and were created to be. It's not something to be taken lightly, and it's not something that can be turned on and off when we please. We must be responsible with it. Another thing you must understand is that sex DOES NOT equal love. Love should always come first. Love takes care of you and your heart, your feelings, your spirit. Sex can make you think you're in love because of the closeness and feelings that it brings but you need to pay attention to what's happening outside of sex. What's going on in your relationship? Does your heart skip a beat when you see him or know that you're going to see him? Does he make you happy? Can he make you smile no matter what is going on in your life? Does he listen to you and accepts you for who you are? To me this is love. Love accepts you, takes care of you and protects you. Love doesn't pressure you into something that could potentially damage your life. Love doesn't make you do things that you know you're not supposed to do. Love is powerful and never ending. You can love someone so much that it takes your breath away. Love at first site may or may not be real, but intense love is. No matter how much you may try to run from it or stuff it away, it's there, and it's deep and all consuming.

If you are led to a guy that has this capability of love, stay and do things God's way! You will not regret it! You will regret not embracing that love. "Fine" or "Sexy" doesn't equate to the ability or level of love or the potential of love. "Fine & sexy" can hurt you and can be a nice cover up of pain and heartache and the inability to love. Be careful and wait for love! Sex without love is nothing but a major life disaster waiting to happen. It cheats you of the beautiful life you were meant to have.

Song of Songs 2:7
Daughters of Jerusalem, I charge you by the gazelles and by the does of the field: Do not arouse or awaken love until it so desires.

1 Corinthians 13 (NIV)
13 If I speak in the tongues[] of men or of angels, but do not have love, I am only a resounding gong or a clanging cymbal. ² If I have the gift of prophecy and can fathom all mysteries and all knowledge, and if I have a faith that can move mountains, but do not have love, I am nothing. ³ If I give all I possess to the poor and give over my body to hardship that I may boast, [] but do not have love, I gain nothing.
⁴ Love is patient, love is kind. It does not envy, it does not boast, it is not proud. ⁵ It does not dishonour others, it is not self-seeking, it is not easily angered, it keeps no record of wrongs. ⁶ Love does not delight in evil but rejoices with the truth. ⁷ It always protects, always trusts, always hopes, always perseveres.
⁸ Love never fails. But where there are prophecies, they will cease; where there are tongues, they will be stilled; where there is knowledge, it will pass away. ⁹ For we know in part and we prophesy in part, ¹⁰ but when completeness comes, what is in part disappears. ¹¹ When I was a child, I talked like a child, I thought like a child, I reasoned like a child. When I became a man, I put the ways of childhood behind me. ¹² For now we see only a reflection as in a mirror; then we shall see face to face. Now I know in part; then I shall know fully, even as I am fully known.
¹³ And now these three remain: faith, hope, and love. But the greatest of these is love.

~Thoughts~

Boundaries

Are you one of those people who hear the word "Bible" and roll your eyes, cringe or run for the hills? I know, I so used to be the same way! That is until I found out what the Bible really is all about. Before I gave my life to Christ, I ran away from anything and anyone who mentioned Jesus, God, Bible, or church. I ran far away. I didn't want to hear about God, certainly didn't know who Jesus was and I didn't want to hear anything about …sin. I didn't realize then that I was running from the One who could rescue me from all that I was battling with.

I thought that by running from God and the Bible, I was keeping my freedom and didn't have to worry about being restricted and constricted. I always thought the Bible was full of words telling me what not to do so that I couldn't have fun and live my life the way I wanted to. I was living life without boundaries. I did whatever I wanted, when I wanted, how I wanted and with whomever I chose to do it with! It took me a long time to learn that the Bible was filled with pages of life-giving words, not life restricting and constricting words. God's word sets boundaries and believe it or not, we certainly do need boundaries!

Without the word of God my life was out-of-bounds and out of control and all that did was allow me to heap loads of pain and heartache on myself! I invited this pain into my life! Not knowing that the whole time I was running from God, He was chasing me with His love and all He wanted to do was protect me, and I wouldn't let Him. God wants to protect us, that's one of the reasons we have the Bible. Let's look at life without the Bible. You must admit; this world is pretty messed up because it chooses not to take heed to the wisdom that's in the Bible. It's not a pretty sight. There's so much pain and evil, all because we'd rather do things our own way. We think we know what's best when really, we don't. God has a huge advantage over us, He sees and knows the future, He knows what's coming and not only that, He created us, so He knows all about us (See Psalm 139). The Word of God is alive and well, and each time we read it, no matter if we've read the same verse several times before, we find exactly what we need for the season that we're in. He knows exactly what we need right when we need it!

We have the wrong view of boundaries. God's boundaries are meant to guide and direct us. If we follow Him, we can have the most amazing life filled with hope and prosperity (Jeremiah 29:11). I mean, why not follow Him? He is the CREATOR of all things so why not go to the ONE who can give us all things? We don't have to work for it, just receive, all because we've given our life over to Him. He loves us beyond measure! Adam & Eve stepped outside of the boundaries God set for them and look what happened? I would say having boundaries set by the Almighty is a pretty awesome idea. To me, it shows just how much He loves and cares for us. Thank you, God for your boundaries!

Psalm 119:11 (NKJV)
Your word I have hidden in my heart,
That I might not sin against You.

~Thoughts~

Who do you think you are?

I was out and about one day (without the kids! Woo hoo!), people watching, and I saw moms dragging their kids and yelling, (which I can relate to) some young girls with shorts up to their butt cheeks, some women in heels I wouldn't dare try to walk down my hallway in let alone the mall, and young girls trying their hardest to get the attention of the young boys there. The thought often comes to my mind, who do we think we are as women? I've found that men respond to us by the way we carry ourselves. If you're dressed like a hooker/prostitute, then you'll be treated like one. In the corporate world, if a woman dresses professionally, she's usually treated with respect. My question to you today is, "Who do you think you are?" Do you think you're beautiful, cute, ugly, fat, and skinny, could lose a few pounds, confident, scary, pitiful? Now, look at the world we live in, scan through some TV channels, who does the world say we need to be? What I see is that we should all be a size 6 or less, have long hair, "beat" our faces, add extra lashes, wear certain clothes by certain designers, go broke to make yourself look as if you're not broke, look like a prostitute to get attention, the list goes on. Well, I choose not to believe those things. I choose to believe what God says about me. Why? Because He created me. I was designed by the greatest designer ever, and so were you! Have you ever thought about who created you? What He has to say about you? What's beautiful in His eyes? Let me help you out:

1. We are fearfully & wonderfully made! (Psalm 139:14)

2. God loves us for who we are! He doesn't look at us the way the world does, He looks at our heart! (1 Samuel 16:7)

3. We are His treasured possessions! (Deuteronomy 26:18)

4. What's important to God is NOT our outward appearance! There is no requirement to be "sexy"! Sexy isn't even in the Bible! God reminds us that beauty comes from our inner self, the unfading beauty of a gentle and quiet spirit. (1 Peter 3:3-4)

5. Hephzibah – this means that God delights in us, takes immense pleasure in us and will claim us as His bride!
Isaiah 62:4 – Never again will you be called "The Forsaken City "or "The Desolate Land. "Your new name will be "The City of God's Delight "and "The Bride of God, "for the Lord delights in you and will claim you as his bride.

Take time to meditate on these truths and then ask yourself, "Who do you think you are?"

~Thoughts~

Attracting Love

There's nothing like a few life changing events to happen to help you to understand what love really is. Getting married, having children, and going through touch experiences with my family have all taught me unconditional love. But the most captivating is the love God has for us. He gave His one and only Son to die for my sinful little behind. Jesus Christ died for me so that I may have life, that I may experience love. That's love! I couldn't imagine seeing my girls dying for anyone on a cross especially for people who didn't want anything to do with love, only their selfish wants, wishes, and desires. Before I came to know the love of Christ, I only *knew of* love. I thought I'd experienced it with random guys from my past, but through Christ, I've learned its true meaning. If I'd know the true meaning before, in the past, I wouldn't have spent my love on those that didn't matter. I would have saved my love for my husband. He deserves all my love, and I want him to have it. I wish that I could have given him the first of everything.

When you are looking for love, you need to first understand that God is love. He's the creator of love. He only knows love. He loves us beyond measure. You should know that you are loved unconditionally through and by Him. Knowing this protects you from looking for love in all the wrong places and from being disappointed time after time after time. Through His love, you will learn that people will fail you and disappoint you, but you will be healed and caught by the love that God has for you. You will need to know God's love for you when you get married. Your husband will be your gift from God, but you must remember that he is human and he will fail, hurt, and disappoint you. But by the grace of God in your marriage, you will not feel any less loved because even in your marriage you will have God's great love.

Marriage requires a deeper love; unconditional love. You will learn to love your husband's greatness as well as his weaknesses and his annoyances. There will be times when he will do something that infuriates you, but because of the love that you have for one another, five minutes later you won't remember it, you will still love each other. You want to attract love, not lust. Lust is fleeting and leaves you empty.

Job 31:11 says "For lust is a shameful sin, a crime that should be punished." You can't build a relationship on something that God considers to be a shameful and criminal act. If you're in a relationship based on lust, what happens when the lust dies, and it will? What will you do then?

When I consider some of my relationships from my past, most of them were based on lust. But once the lust died, I found out he was only after one thing and underneath that lust was nothing of substance to build a relationship on so, on to the next guy. It's a never ending, ugly, vicious cycle of nothingness and pain. The act of lustful dating is a setup from the enemy to sabotage your future. I say this because, in marriage, there will be times that you lust after your husband and that's good because it keeps your sex life alive, but then there will be times when you don't, and your marriage must be steeped in love to withstand the times when the lust/desire has temporarily waned.

So how do you attract love and not lust? I truly believe that you attract what you are. If you are a loving person and have a loving personality, I believe that's what you will attract if you don't settle. Do you speak words of love? Are your words and actions that which exude love? Men watch our personalities and actions. They treat you the way that you treat and carry yourself. Act like a slut, get treated like one. Act as if you deserve less than the best, then that is what you will get. A woman's motives show in her actions and her eyes. A guy can pick up on your whole story based on your actions and so can another woman. You attract what and who you are and not just with men but in all your relationships. If you're attracting everything but what you want, check your heart! What are you giving off?

1 Peter 3:3-5 Don't be concerned about the outward beauty of fancy hairstyles, expensive jewelry, or beautiful clothes. You should clothe yourselves instead with the beauty that comes from within, the unfading beauty of a gentle and quiet spirit, which is so precious to God. This is how the holy women of old made themselves beautiful. They trusted God and accepted the authority of their husbands.

~Thoughts~

Re-View Your Body

There's so much pressure on us as women to conform to the standards of what we see in the media. Whether it's in our career choice, to be a mom or not to be, to work or not to work, be skinny, don't be fat, etc. We feel the pressure to fit the world's definition of a highly successful, powerful woman, you know, be "normal". The way the world operates and defines beauty is the total opposite of what God defines as beautiful. We are making the "rulers" of this world rich by buying into the lies that if you buy this product and that product you will feel better, look better, find your man, guaranteed! Insert eye roll here! Not so! In Psalm 139 verse 14, states that we are fearfully and wonderfully made". *Dictionary.com defines fearful as "full of awe or reverence" and wonderful as "excellent; great; marvelous. Of a sort that causes or arouse wonder; amazing; astonishing."* Wow! Have you ever thought or looked at your body this way? I mean, our bodies, especially as women, can do amazing things and have amazing power. The sad part is that this power is being misused and this misuse is destroying our lives. God's word does not say that we are horribly and wrongly made, it says that we are fearfully and wonderfully made. There's nothing wrong with us. We have made it up in our minds that there's something wrong because we have allowed our minds to be programmed to think that what we see in the mirror is wrong and what we see on TV and in magazines is right. Romans 12:2 tells us, "And do not be conformed to this world, but be transformed by the renewing of your mind, that you may prove what is that good and acceptable and perfect will of God". Now, it is our responsibility to take care of this wonderful body that we've been given and sometimes we don't do a fantastic job of this. I am guilty of this for sure, but we must remember that our bodies house the Spirit of the Lord, our body is His temple (1 Corinthians 6:19). The next time you think of mistreating your body or disrespecting it in any way, think of Who lives in you.

So, what's the remedy for this wrong thinking? Reviewing our body. If we've been wonderfully made by the creator, then we need to accept this truth! It is the truth because God said it and God cannot and will not lie. According to God's word, we have the power to change our mind, to renew our mind and take our thoughts captive and bring them into His truth (2 Corinthians 10:5). You are your thoughts, that's why in Philippians 4:8 we are told to think on whatever is pure, lovely, admirable, excellent, and praiseworthy. Thinking of our bodies as wrong, hideous, or ugly is incorrect thinking, and we need to change that. God made us each unique. Most of all, God knows who your future husband is and what he likes. Has it ever occurred to you that the way your body is shaped, your curves, the size of your behind, tummy, and breast, even your skin, is exactly what your future husband is looking for? God has all of this worked out, but if you don't love, respect and cherish your body, then why should anyone else? Be secure in who you are and in the fact that you know God took the time to create your wonderful, precious body and He loves every inch of what He created. In Genesis 1:31, it says that God saw all that he had made and it was very good! (Emphasis mine)

~Thoughts~

Dare to be Different! ♡♡

Dare to be different! Dare to be who God has created you to be, His Beloved! Not some man's whore, sex object or toy. Not some man's punching bag, security blanket, or caretaker. Not someone for him to abuse, misuse, mistreat, neglect. You were created for more!

Dare to walk in the confidence of knowing that you're loved beyond measure, beyond comparison, beyond comprehension! Dare to be a virgin and be proud to be one! Dare to be celibate and save yourself for your future husband. Dare to wait and keep yourself pure and holy!

Dare to be different and cover yourself! Dare to dress modestly and not cause your brother to sin from looking at you! Causing him to commit adultery in his mind and heart because you feel you should look "sexy" to attract his attention. If he is attracted to you because the way you dress suggests that you're going to give him exactly what he's thinking, then what does that say about you?

Dare to live out God's truth. Dare to bask in the awesome knowledge that you're fearfully and wonderfully made! Knowing and walking in God's truth is power, freedom, and peace! This world does not love you and never will!

Dare to trust God to give you all that He has for you, more than you could ever imagine! Dare to trust him with all you are and have, and you'll never be disappointed!

                Dare to be Different!

~Thoughts~

Jesus

John 10:10 NKJ
The thief does not come except to steal, and to kill, and to destroy. I have come that they may have life and that they may have it more abundantly.

Who's Your Hubby?

Is one of your greatest hopes, dreams, wishes…marriage? Finding the perfect hubby, having the perfect kids, perfect family? Well, what if… God's plan is for you to stay single? What if His plans to prosper you and give you hope and a future (Jeremiah 29:11) <u>does not</u> include marriage? To never marry a man, never have sex, but to be forever married to Him only?

We are all married to Him if we have surrendered our lives to Him, but what if you are not supposed to marry, could you handle that? Are you in a place in your life right now where you could say that you have totally surrendered all your hopes, wishes, and dreams to God and trust that whatever He has for you, you know that it's for your good, He will see you through it, and you will ultimately be satisfied with it if you keep your eyes on Him? Or have you become so engrossed with the picture of marriage and sex that the thought of letting go of that dream and trusting God with it makes you want to break down and cry?! Even as a married woman, I still have to lie all my hopes, wishes, and dreams down at His feet and say, Lord, not my will, but yours! Married, single, widowed, divorced, we still should trust Him and fight for our purity, fight to stay faithful to Him and His Word. Trusting His unconditional, undying, indescribable, all-encompassing love for us! Honestly, I feel as if I need Him more now in marriage and as a mom than I ever have! It's not easy being married and I know that it's not easy being single but see when I was single, I didn't know God, not like I know Him now. If I knew Him then like I know Him now, I would have known my worth, how loved I am and how precious, beautiful, and awesome I was and am in Him and to Him! I'm not saying that you won't have days where the hormones won't try to take over, but at least you know that you have God and He will help you to deal with those hormones, urges, and temptations. Now, if you have not surrendered your life to Jesus then, unfortunately, you are left to fight those battles on your own, and as a woman who had the experience of fighting the battles on her own, and lost, I'm telling you, you will lose! Life is messy and crazy, and without God, it's downright scary! I couldn't go back to a life without Him; He's just too good to me! He is still my husband, and He loves me in ways that my husband in his human nature is incapable of. So, husband or not, you will still be married to God, the lover of your soul, and that's not an unpleasant situation to be in at all.

Psalm 117:2 NLT
For he loves us with unfailing LOVE; the LORD's faithfulness endures forever. Praise the LORD!

Matthew 22:37 NLT
Jesus replied, 'You
must LOVE THE LORD YOUR GOD WITH ALL YOUR heart, all your soul, and all your mind.'

Jeremiah 31:3 NLT
Long ago the LORD said to Israel: "I have loved you, my people, with an everlasting LOVE. With unfailing LOVE, I have drawn you to myself.

Psalm 130:7 NLT
O Israel, hope in the LORD; for with the LORD, there is unfailing LOVE. His redemption overflows.

1 Chronicles 16:34 NLT
   Give thanks to the LORD, for he is good! His faithful LOVE endures forever.

~Thoughts~

Drop Your Bags!

One of the goals of teaching women God's truth about sex and purity is so that they'll have the freedom to release all their baggage. Jesus came and died on the cross to take on all our mess from our past mistakes and remove the weight from us. Then it hit me; we need to drop our bags! Drop all of it at His feet and keep it moving –forward! Lot's wife was turned into a pillar of salt for looking back at sin filled Sodom & Gomorrah (Genesis 19:26)! God wants us to trust Him and the awesome plan He has for our future (Jeremiah 29:11). He never meant for us to carry so much pain and heartache in the first place. Not only does carrying around baggage hurt us, but it also hurts our relationships and marriages. When we leave a messy and unhealthy relationship or situation, we often make the mistake of bringing baggage with us and dumping it all on the new guy who genuinely wants to love us and do right by us. Also, in marriages, which I found to be true in mine, all the pain of past sexual experiences almost destroyed my chance at enjoying the beautiful gift of sex with my husband. Just simply not knowing God's truth about sex can destroy our marriages because we're taught that sex is shameful, nasty, and wrong and that's so not true! My dear sisters, drop the bags! Only keep the cute ones that match your outfits. Get rid of the ones labelled: **selfish, self-sufficient, so I don't need a man, control freak, insecure, I don't trust anyone**…see where I'm going with this? Sometimes these traits come as a form of an unhealthy defence mechanism which only ends up hurting us. God is close to the broken-hearted, and He heals all our hurts and wounds. Don't hold on to the bags!

Savin' It for Hubby is not just about saving sex for your hubby but your heart, emotions, and love as well. He deserves to have it first (after God of course). Remove yourself from situations that you know are not good for you. If it's been years and he still can't decide or get himself together, move on, and leave the mess with him, don't bring it with you to stink up what you may have with Mr. Right. If you're single, wait and let Jesus be your husband. He's the best husband there is!

~Thoughts~

The Rib

Genesis
2:20 So the man gave names to all the livestock, the birds in the sky and all the wild animals. But for Adam, no suitable helper was found. 21 So the Lord God caused the man to fall into a deep sleep; and while he was sleeping, he took one of the man's ribs and then closed the place with flesh. 22 Then the Lord God made a woman from the rib he had taken out of the man, and he brought her to the man.

The purpose of the ribs/rib cage in the human body is to protect the heart and lungs, two of the most vital organs in the body.
Even though the rib cage has a big job of protecting these vital internal organs, the ribs themselves are easily broken. When I think of women and the fact that God formed us from the rib of man, I think of our purpose as women and, how life outside of God can break us. I was prompted to find out more about the "rib", wife, protector of heart and home and my research helped me to understand why women are not rejoicing in the
peace, unconditional love, and freedom that we have in Jesus Christ. Other than the fact that you must first surrender your life to Christ, my research on the purpose of the rib in the human body revealed some surprising discoveries that are so relative to God's reason and purposes for us to save ourselves for our husbands.

1. **The rib/rib cage is one of the toughest and most painful areas to treat if any of the ribs become broken.** God created us as the softer side, the more nurturing side of men. When we are in a relationship, we automatically open to him fully, and the urge to be open to him physically

comes naturally. But, when we open ourselves up prematurely to the wrong person, the one we're not married to, we open ourselves up to the possibility of being hurt and broken. When a woman is hurt, it's hard to bounce back. Even more so when you've given yourself to this man, mind, **body,** and soul. When you finally get rid of the wrong person, it's hard for the new and right person to gain your trust and everything that the wrong person did, all the baggage that's left behind hinders your relationship with Mr. Right and even God. You're kind of expecting the next guy to do the same things the others did to hurt you or betray your trust. Treating this broken "rib" is tough; it's often a painful and long recovery. We find ourselves trying to recover from something that God has already warned us about and never intended for us to experience.

2. ***Fractured ribs can cause excruciating pain.*** A woman who has gone through some painful things in her life can cause excruciating pain to others; hurt/hurting people, hurt people. I know that the things in my life that have hurt me, my mom being on drugs, multiple relationships with men and the heart breaks, caused pain in my marriage, to my husband. For the record, my dear sisters, what you do now will have a significant impact on your marriage! I was so hurt and damaged and had so much baggage from my past that it almost ruined my marriage. I am so grateful to God today for healing! When I met my husband, I thought he was just like the rest of the "garbage" I'd dealt with and had been lugging around for all those years, but thank God that he stuck around and was able to see and love me despite and through the process of me getting rid of the baggage!

3. ***Sharp, intense pain is indicative of a broken rib along with difficulty breathing, moving, or touching the tender area.*** Have you ever been so hurt by someone that it felt as if your heart would literally break, explode, or fall out of your chest?

It hurts to breathe, to move on with your life or to let anyone in. I have experienced this pain on numerous occasions. Most from past relationships and then when my mom died a month after I had my first daughter. My wonderful sisters, the only Way and only One that can heal this type of pain is God, our Lord and Savior Jesus Christ! Not another new outfit, a new pair of shoes, new haircut, and definitely not a new relationship! Remember from Genesis 2:22 that God brought Eve to Adam, so you don't have to go on a man hunt! When the time is right, God will do what He does best and work things out smoothly, but as women we must trust Him to do this or else we will be trying to dig ourselves out of mess and if we're so covered in mess, how can we expect God to bring us to anyone or anything that we've prayed for?

Psalm 34: 18-20 he delivers them from all their troubles. The Lord is close to the brokenhearted and saves those who are crushed in spirit. The righteous person may have many troubles, but the Lord delivers him from them all; he protects all his <u>bones, not one of them will be broken. (Emphasis mine)</u>

God was very serious about his reasons and purposes for creating sex for married couples only. Sex is His wedding gift/blessing to married couples-male & female. He warned of the consequences of having sex outside of marriage. He knew of the pain, heartaches, heartbreaks, and brokenness that it would cause. So, if you're hurting, let God be the next relationship you look to for comfort, to give you love, heal and to adore you!

~Thoughts~

He Does That for Me?

Psalm 8:4 WHAT IS MAN THAT YOU ARE MINDFUL OF HIM, THE SON OF MAN THAT YOU CARE FOR HIM?

In this passage of scripture, the word "mindful" really stuck out to me, so I looked it up in the dictionary, and these three phrases from the definition of the word coupled with this scripture brought me life:

1. A*ttentive of/to* - God is attentive to our **needs, wants, and desires** (HE KNOWS ABOUT OUR SEXUAL DESIRES, AND YES, HE WILL HELP YOU WITH THOSE AS WELL, JUST ASK GOD TO HELP YOU TO STAY PURE AND TRUST HIM!). He knows us inside and out, and He knows what we need before we even ask. (Psalm 139 & Matthew 6:25-34)
2. **AWARE OF** – God is aware of what's going on in our hearts, minds, and our lives. He delights (takes pleasure in) in every little detail of our lives! He cares about how tired we are, what's bothering us, what makes us happy and laugh and what makes us sad and cry.
3. **CAREFUL OF** – God is also cautious and thorough when it comes to us. He makes sure that we're taken care of and that He doesn't give us things too hastily, only in His perfect timing. He knows us so well and knows how we will respond to things, good and bad. He protects us, soothes, and calms us and most importantly He loves and cherishes us! He loves us enough to say no or not right now, and He loves us enough to bless us as well!

Our Father is mindful of us, regardless of what we've done in the past, or how we messed up yesterday or in the last 5 minutes, He is still right beside us, attending to us!

~Thoughts~

Trust Me!

Ever had a week that seemed as if it was specially delivered to you from hell, personally? Warfare from all angles? I have! What happened, you ask? Well for one, I fought with my husband, yelled at my kids, and got discouraged about my calling, future and my purpose for being on this Earth. Why did all this happen to me? Well once I had a moment to really listen to God and really think about what was going on, I realized that I'd stopped trusting God and somehow along the way started putting my trust in myself. I listened to the lies of the enemy. I let him side swipe me and take away the wonderful word that I'd received from God the week before. The enemy sucker punched me right in the gut! My revelation came at church the following weekend. Wouldn't you know it, the sermon was "How a Woman Should Respect a Man". All I could think was, oh boy, here we go. I was still upset with hubby about our previous argument. Anyway, I'm listening, and I had the biggest chip of pride and defensiveness on my shoulder! Ugh! I listened, and my pastor said something that was like a light bulb going off big time in my head and my heart:

1 Peter 3:1-6 wives, in the same way, submit yourselves to your own husbands so that, if any of them do not believe the word, they may be won over without words by the behavior of their wives, 2 when they see the purity and reverence of your lives. 3 your beauty should not come from outward adornments, such as elaborate hairstyles and the wearing of gold jewelry or fine clothes. 4 rather, it should be that of your inner self, the unfading beauty of a gentle and quiet spirit, which is of great worth in god's sight. 5 for this is the way the holy women of the past who put their hope in god used to adorn themselves. They submitted themselves to their own husbands, 6 like Sarah, who obeyed Abraham and called him her lord. You are her daughters if you do what is right and do not give way to fear.

Now, for my single sisters, there will be times in marriage where you will want to run for the hills, fight your husband, punch him, you won't agree with the decision that he's come up with and you fear disaster coming, but what we all must remember is that even though we're married to a man, we're still married to God. That's how I see it. He will always be our husband. Anyway, my pastor said that we must obey God, not fear our husbands but trust that God has our backs no matter how the situation looks or how we feel. Regardless of what's going on or what we think or feel, we are to respect our husbands and trust that God is in the midst. Then it hit me, all my trouble came when I stopped trusting God and started listening to lies and trusting my little weak self instead! No wonder I was a mess by the end of the week! I gave way to fear, just what the word said NOT to do. You can't have a successful marriage or relationship without God. It's not going to happen. If I know nothing else, I know that I must have a relationship with God. My husband and I would not be married now if we didn't have God in our marriage. Marriage is WORK! You must die to yourself daily. Once you say, "I do" get ready to fight because you've officially ticked the enemy off. Marriage is instituted by God. It mirrors the intimate relationship He wishes to have with us. The Bible says that he who finds a wife finds what is good and **RECEIVES FAVOR FROM THE LORD** (Proverbs 18:22). Guess who doesn't like that? Guess who's going to be one of the enemy's main targets? You, dear sister. Before you get married, you must have a strong relationship with Christ. Your marriage depends on it. Make sure you trust God to bring you to the strong man of God that He has for you. Trust God!

When I pray and ask God questions about what I should do about things, sometimes the only answer I get is "Trust Me", or He will ask "do you trust Me?" and I say yes and that's it. We walk by faith not by sight and if your faith is not rooted in Him and your trust isn't in Him, get ready to be side swiped!

Hubby and I made up, I repented, and I have my peace back, but one thing's for sure, I will make every effort to keep my eyes on Him and that I'm trusting Him all the way, no matter how things look, or how I feel!

~Thoughts~

Trusting God's Plan for Your Life

When things are looking up in our lives, and our plans are going the way we want or better, it's easy to trust God and praise Him. We don't get shaken until things start to go wrong. This is when it takes more of an effort to trust God's perfect plan. This is what puts our faith to work. When I think about trusting God's plan for my life, I often question the milestones throughout the journey. What is it about trusting God's plan for our lives that almost brings about a sense of dread? For me, it's because I never know what trials or tests I'm going to face! It's uncomfortable and uncertain. Isn't it just like us to want to know the end before we've begun? With God, it's all about the journey, not just the destination. It's in the journey, in the everyday walking and living that we become prepared for the result, the blessing. God may or may not tell us or show us our purpose, or our destiny up front, but just as Abraham modeled, we must go. God doesn't always tell us how to get there, He just leads us to take the first step.

God is purposeful; He uses everything to shape, mold and prepare us for our destiny. He even uses our frustrations. Our frustration comes from not getting what we want, when and how we want it. Again, it's all about the journey. Take David for instance. In the end, He was "a man after God's own heart" and loved by many. In the beginning, he was an overlooked, underestimated shepherd boy! How often do we feel overlooked and underestimated? But to our immense joy, our God doesn't look at the outer appearance, He looks at the heart (1 Samuel 16:7 NIV).

David, a shepherd boy, knows that he will be king one day, but he doesn't go directly to being king. God proceeds to move in David's life and orchestrates situations and circumstances that begin to train and prepare David for kingship. By being humble, faithful, and obedient to God, David not only defeats Goliath and Saul but wins over the hearts of his people. Did this happen overnight? No. Did it happen the way David may have wanted or thought it should have happened? No. But, in David's journey, he became what God created him to be. Was David perfect? Not by a long shot! He experienced several personal failures along the way, especially his affair with Bathsheba after he became king!

Now, what can we learn from our brother David?

1. He knew his purpose but had to endure some tests and trials along his journey to reaching his destiny.

2. He didn't reach his destiny overnight.

3. He had to deal with haters and threats on his life, but he trusted God and kept going despite.

4. He had some mountain top experiences and some valley experiences, but he trusted what God said and kept his focus on his journey to becoming king.

5. Even when he reached his destiny, he still messed up. Reaching your destiny doesn't make all your problems, issues or temptations go away, you just have new ones! We must keep growing.

6. Throughout his journey, David trusted God's plan for his life despite the adversity.

Don't get discouraged when things don't go as planned or your destiny seems to get further away instead of you getting closer to it. Keep going and trust God in your journey. Restore your faith in Him for your life!

~Thoughts~

The Importance of Being in His Presence Daily

Have you ever tried walking around your home in the dark and you think you know what piece of furniture is where from memory and then you bump into something and hurt yourself? Then you think, how'd that get there or who moved this?! This is how I see myself when I don't start my day with God when I haven't spent time in His presence. I feel as if I'm walking in the dark, groping around trying to find my own way by what I think I know to be true but isn't always the case. All the while the enemy is moving things around to trip me and bump into me throughout the day.

I used to think that I could just say 'GOOD MORNING LORD, PLEASE BE WITH ME THROUGHOUT THIS DAY' and that would be fine. By the end of the day, I would be stressed out and stretched thin. Starting with God helps me to acknowledge the fact that "APART FROM HIM, I CAN DO NOTHING!" (John 15:5 NIV84). The best thing is not only starting with Him but having His spirit and guidance throughout the day as well. God is my best friend; I can tell Him everything, good, bad, and just plain ugly! He listens, understands, and helps you through!

I remember a day I had when nothing went right! I woke up late and just couldn't get my thoughts together. I had to change my eye shadow twice, changed my hair twice, changed clothes at least three times; I was rushing my daughter to get ready for school, and I was running behind schedule getting lunches packed. I get to work, finally, and still couldn't function. It took an extra effort just to work and concentrate on what I was doing! I couldn't figure out what was going on with me. I figured that maybe I was just having an off day; after all, we have those from time to time. But then I started thinking, what's really going on with me today? Then I remembered that I hadn't spent any time at all with God that morning! None, I just hit the ground running! Well, no wonder I couldn't function, I hadn't had my intimate time with my "EVER-PRESENT HELP IN TIME OF TROUBLE" (Psalm 46:1).

I'm not saying you should get up before the rooster crows and spend three hours reading and praying unless you want to, but spend SOME time with Him, talk to Him. Have coffee or tea with Him. Tell Him your hopes and dreams, needs and wants for this day and listen to Him as He guides and loves on you. He already knows what we need; He just wants to have a relationship with us. (Matthew 6:8 NIV84). God desires that we seek Him as much as we need Him!

BEING IN HIS PRESENCE DAILY:

1. **GIVES US PEACE!** Peace in knowing that even though we don't know what the day is going to bring, He does! Since we have a relationship with Him, He will be with us and direct our paths! We don't have to figure it all out for He says, *"I will instruct you and teach you in the way you should go; I will counsel you and watch over you"* (Psalm 32:8 NIV84). We don't have to know all the answers, He does, and we must trust Him! *"Trust in the Lord with all your heart and lean not on*

your own understanding; in all your ways acknowledge him, and he will make your paths straight" (Proverbs 3:5-6 NIV84).

2. **WE GET HIS BEST FOR OUR DAY!** *"This is what the Lord says— your Redeemer, the Holy One of Israel: "I am the Lord your God, who teaches you what is best for you, who directs you in the way you should go"* (Isaiah 48:17 NIV84).

3. **WE GET WISDOM, GUIDANCE, AND DIRECTION.** *"But I'll take the hand of those who don't know the way, who can't see where they're going. I'll be a personal guide to them, directing them through unknown country. I'll be right there to show them what roads to take, make sure they don't fall into the ditch. These are the things I'll be doing for them— sticking with them, not leaving them for a minute"* (Isaiah 42:16 MSG). If this isn't comforting, then I don't know what is! These are the words of God, our Father! Can you imagine Him saying this to you every morning?

4. **WE GET PROTECTION FROM THE ENEMY'S PLANS TO TRIP US UP, DISCOURAGE US, OR TO TAKE OUR EYES OFF GOD.** *"If you make the Most High your dwelling—even the Lord, who is my refuge—then no harm will befall you, no disaster will come near your tent. For he will command his angels concerning you to guard you in all your ways; they will lift you up in their hands, so that you will not strike your foot against a stone. You will tread upon the lion and the cobra; you will trample the great lion and the serpent. "Because he loves me," says the Lord, "I will rescue him; I will protect him, for he acknowledges my name. He will call upon me, and I will*

answer him; I will be with him in trouble, I will deliver him and honor him." (Psalm 91:9-15)

5. **WE GET HIS UNDIVIDED ATTENTION, LOVE, AND DEVOTION!** (Jeremiah 31:3 NIV84) *"The Lord appeared to us in the past, saying: "I have loved you with an everlasting love; I have drawn you with loving-kindness."*

Being in His presence daily is vital for us as His children. We can't make it without Him. We can't fight this battle without Him; we're not strong enough and most of all He sees what we can't!

He loves us so much and wants to take care of us, why not bask in His presence? You'll be so glad you did!

~Thoughts~

God's Perfect Timing

Romans 8:28 and we know that in all things god works for the good of those who love him, who have been called according to his purpose.

This was the hardest for me to accept. I know that God's timing is His way of protecting me, preparing me but it's the whole dying to myself thing that makes it so hard! Giving over everything to Him; my hopes, dreams, wishes and wants to Him, entrusting Him with all things. Knowing that He is working them all out, every single thing. We must remember that he is the giver of all good things and everything He promises does and will come to pass and not fail (Joshua 23:14). In our eyes and mind, we have it all worked out. We have a fool-proof plan of how our life should be; when things should happen and how. I often wonder what God is saying to us when we say, "God, I got the rest if you just let XYZ happen." But even in this He loves us and says, "Father knows best!" I'm so glad that He does! I'm so glad that He has my best interests at heart! I'm so glad that He protects me! Grateful for grace and mercy! It's not that we're not supposed to have hopes and dreams, but we are called to trust His timing and wait for Him. Psalm 37:4 states that if we delight ourselves in the Lord that he will give us the desires of our hearts. So, instead of getting all anxious and rattled because it seems as if our lives are falling apart, how about we rest in His peace and trust that His greatest is coming to us!

Scriptures for encouragement: Joshua 23:14, Jeremiah 29:11, Psalm 37:4-7a, Proverbs 3:5, Proverbs 16:3, Proverbs 19:21

~Thoughts~

Keep Your Eyes on the Prize

MATTHEW 14:26-32
26 WHEN THE DISCIPLES SAW HIM WALKING ON THE LAKE, THEY WERE TERRIFIED. "IT'S A GHOST," THEY SAID, AND CRIED OUT IN FEAR. 27 BUT JESUS IMMEDIATELY SAID TO THEM: "TAKE COURAGE! IT IS I. DON'T BE AFRAID." 28 "LORD, IF IT'S YOU," PETER REPLIED, "TELL ME TO COME TO YOU ON THE WATER." 29 "COME," HE SAID. THEN PETER GOT DOWN OUT OF THE BOAT, WALKED ON THE WATER AND CAME TOWARD JESUS. 30 BUT WHEN HE SAW THE WIND, HE WAS AFRAID AND, BEGINNING TO SINK, CRIED OUT, "LORD, SAVE ME!" 31 IMMEDIATELY JESUS REACHED OUT HIS HAND AND CAUGHT HIM. "YOU OF LITTLE FAITH," HE SAID, "WHY DID YOU DOUBT?" 32 AND WHEN THEY CLIMBED INTO THE BOAT, THE WIND DIED DOWN.

When I think about keeping my focus on Jesus, I always think about Peter walking on the water. I try to put myself in his place and picture how I would react and what I would do. First comes the fear of the unknown and the leap of faith and trust but then on my journey of faith and trust, things get a little scary and uncomfortable. And we all love to be comfortable, right? Or, things can get too comfortable, and we start to think that we're in control and that we don't need any help, we got this! Yeah, right! Anyway, back to my story, so I'm walking towards Jesus, and then I start to look around at my surroundings, and my circumstances and situations and I start to sink mentally, physically, emotionally, and spiritually. When we start to look at our problems, circumstances, and situations instead of Jesus and His Promises, we give the enemy a little victory. His goal is to steal our affections from Christ. The enemy and his cronies begin to party because they're enjoying our misery! And why is this happening? Because we thought we had it going on, got comfortable and we take our eyes off our map, didn't listen to our GPS, and we go the wrong way or start looking at our stuff more than we are looking at Jesus.

Then, we cry out and realize He was there the whole time, it was us who decided to take our eyes off Him. It's hard to focus when we're in pain, when we're afraid when we don't know what's going on, but we must keep our eyes on Jesus. How do we do that? By studying His Word and staying in constant contact with Him throughout our day. Take Him with you wherever you go. Tell Him everything that you're feeling, that you're going through. It's not as if He doesn't know what's going on; it's building a solid relationship and foundation with Him. He doesn't force us into a relationship with Him, He welcomes us. By doing this, we won't sink!

~Thoughts~

Chosen!

EPHESIANS 1:4 FOR HE CHOSE US IN HIM BEFORE THE CREATION OF THE WORLD TO BE HOLY AND BLAMELESS IN HIS SIGHT. (NIV)

I don't by any means consider myself better than anyone else because I am a sinner, saved and forgiven. I still mess up, make mistakes, I sin. But, when I read the above scripture, I'm baffled and am in awe of the love that God has for me, for us. In me trying to understand this awesome love, this is what I've learned:

1. God **CHOSE** us in him. Our little sinful behinds! When you think of all the things you've done wrong in your life and all the wrong things you've said or thought, the fact that God would even think to choose us despite our many shortcomings, remarkable!

2. *Before* THE CREATION OF THE WORLD. Before he created the world in all its splendor and glory, he chose us to be in him, with him, of him, before anything else, he *chose* us!

3. TO BE *holy and blameless* IN HIS SIGHT. We were *chosen* to be **HOLY AND BLAMELESS**. Keyword again, **CHOSEN**. Meaning there's no way we can be **HOLY AND BLAMELESS** on our own and God knows that yet He still **CHOSE** us!

How can you NOT love a God like this? How can you NOT want to surrender your life to a loving, wonderful, forgiving God who relentlessly loves us and pursues us? Yet we would rather run from him because we think that we're beyond ever being **HOLY AND BLAMELESS**. Well, guess what? We are not beyond being **HOLY AND BLAMELESS** because we were **CHOSEN** IN HIM to be! You can't live this life without Him. Life is so much better with Him!

~Thoughts~

Always Come Back to This

JEREMIAH 29:11-13 11 FOR I KNOW THE PLANS I HAVE FOR YOU," DECLARES THE LORD, "PLANS TO PROSPER YOU AND NOT TO HARM YOU, PLANS TO GIVE YOU HOPE AND A FUTURE.12 THEN YOU WILL CALL UPON ME AND COME AND PRAY TO ME, AND I WILL LISTEN TO YOU.13 YOU WILL SEEK ME AND FIND ME WHEN YOU SEEK ME WITH ALL YOUR HEART. (NIV)

When things in my life seem crazy, and I don't understand what's going on, I always come back to this scripture. This helps me to come back to the fact that God knows what He's doing. He created me, and He has plans for me. His plans, unlike mine, are not to harm me and to give me hope and a future. My plans, however, usually end in a big mess! God can see the bigger picture that we can't see. He has His reasons for saying no to some things and yes to others. All we can think is God why didn't you answer my prayers in the way in which I asked because I already have everything worked out in my mind according to the little view that I have?

I was in my twenties when I'd found out God's truth about sex, and by then it was too late. I'd already had sex multiple times with different guys. God says to wait because He knows why He created sex and by us having sex outside of marriage, we totally abuse and go against everything sex stands for. Sex outside of marriage is outside of the will of God because it goes against His word, which isn't in His plans for us.

He also says that His plans are to prosper us and not to harm us. I take this to mean that we don't have to work ourselves to death to gain wealth and we don't have to do anything that demeans our value or worth. Our worth and value are found in Jesus Christ our Lord and Savior, not in giving our bodies away to the highest bidder! Prostitution and stripping are not God's way for us. God loves and treasures us as women! And, prostitution and stripping don't just happen in a club. We do this by compromising our morals in several areas such as business, ministry, work life, and just trying to get ahead! We strip away all that has been poured into us by God!

Sex may be in the plans that God has for you, but in His timing. When we rush and go against God's purpose and timing, we mess things up and miss out on or delay the wonderful blessings that He has for our future. Something else I love about this passage of scripture is that we can come to God and pray to Him and He will listen! Not might listen, but He will listen. I must remind myself of this from time to time because some of the things we go through in life hurt us so badly and the only One who can do anything about it is God. When He doesn't answer when we want Him to in the way we want Him to, we have the tendency to doubt whether He was listening at all in the first place. Something to understand about God is, He can't lie, and His Word does not come back to Him void, it comes to do what He meant for it to do. So, if you can't trust anyone and have no one to go to, God is and will always be there. He also says that when we seek Him, we will find Him when we seek Him with all our heart. Meaning, He must become everything to you. Seems kind of hefty but it's not, it's freeing. Loving God and surrendering everything to Him gives us freedom. He gives us the peace that we need to get through the darkest and most painful events in our lives. When God is everything, loving yourself comes easier because He accepts us for who we are. Loving God and giving ourselves fully to Him teaches us to love others and prepares us to love our future husbands and children.

Until we are married, God is our husband, He's everything that we don't have and everything we do and will ever need! Oh, how well do I know how it feels to say, "God if I just had this thing or that person I'd be ok" but we must think about why do we want this thing or that person and figure out why we think things or a person will fill a void and what void are we trying to fill. What I've come to learn is that no thing or person will ever fill all your needs or wants, ever. People are not capable, and things are temporary. There will be voids in our lives that only God can fill. That's why after having sex outside of marriage, you still feel empty inside as if something is missing. In Genesis, God brought Eve to Adam. Eve didn't have to go having sex with several guys to find Adam. Eve didn't have to do anything but just be Eve, and God did the rest! We must trust God when He says that He knows the future He has for us, and we must stick to our part of seeking Him with all our hearts and surrendering everything to Him. Even in marriage, God is still everything to me. My husband is human and can only do so much, and my beautiful children can only fill so much of my heart but the rest of me is filled by God in ways that only He can, and for that, I am truly grateful!

~Thoughts~

What's Really Important to God?

Isaiah 3:16-4:1 (AMP)

16 Moreover, the Lord said, Because the daughters of Zion are haughty and walk with outstretched necks and with undisciplined (flirtatious and alluring) eyes, tripping along with mincing and affected gait, and making a tinkling noise with [the anklets on] their feet,

17 Therefore the Lord will smite with a scab the crown of the heads of the daughters of Zion [making them bald], and the Lord will cause them to be [taken as captives and to suffer the indignity of being] stripped naked.

18 In that day the Lord will take away the finery of their tinkling anklets, the caps of network, the crescent head ornaments,

19 The pendants, the bracelets or chains, and the spangled face veils and scarfs,

20 The headbands, the short ankle chains [attached from one foot to the other to ensure a measured gait], the sashes, the perfume boxes, the amulets, or charms [suspended from the ears or neck],

21 The signet rings and nose rings,

22 The festal robes, the cloaks, the stoles and shawls, and the handbags,

23 The hand mirrors, the fine linen [undergarments], the turbans, and the [whole body-enveloping] veils.

24 And it shall come to pass that instead of the sweet odor of spices there shall be the stench of rottenness; and instead of a girdle, a rope; and instead of well-set hair, baldness; and instead

of a rich robe, a girding of sackcloth; and searing [of captives by the scorching heat] instead of beauty.
25 Your men shall fall by the sword, and your mighty men in battle.
26 And [Jerusalem's] gates shall lament and mourn [as those who wail for the dead]; and she, being ruined and desolate, shall sit upon the ground.
And in that day [a]seven women shall take hold of one man, saying, We will eat our own bread and provide our own apparel; only let us be called by your name to take away our reproach [of being unmarried].

I could spend time on what's happening before these verses, but I feel that the verses themselves say enough! When I first read this, my mouth dropped open! This is so much of what we see in the world and church today concerning us ladies! We do love our jewelry, clothes, getting our hair and nails done, you know "taking care of ourselves." But, are we really taking care of ourselves or are we trying to cover something up? Yes, we want to look good, but if we look around and then really look at ourselves, we must ask what's really going on with us women? Is the shopping for these things excessive? Are you living beyond your means in trying to keep up with the latest fashions? Why so many "things"? In this passage, what strikes me most is how true this is for today. Right down to the way that we walk when we're trying to get the attention of a nice-looking man. The way we make eye contact with a guy, you know, that "I want you" look or that "look at me" look. What are we doing here? We're seeking attention, right? Ok, attention from whom? Men! Not God's attention, but the attention of men. There's no limit these days to what a woman will do to get a man. All of which has nothing to do with glorifying God. All with the notion of getting a man, getting our needs met or being affirmed because we didn't get it from our fathers, the list is endless. But the problem is, we're going about it the wrong way. We need Jesus! Not a man. Man can only do so much, only Jesus can fill that void that you're trying to fill doing stuff that you'll regret later! Moving on to verse 17, God begins the process of stripping away "things". Starting with the hair, His goal is to reveal and uncover the secret parts, to strip everything down, having nothing to hide behind. No fly hair-dos, no expensive clothing that the world says we should have. No expensive jewelry, bags and purses, and other accessories; everything taken away. Now, let's look at what's left. Look at your heart for a moment. What's going on inside there? When all the make-up and eyelashes, jewelry, shoes, clothes, hair-dos, and bags are gone, what do you see? Are you happy with what you see? Are you at peace with yourself, with God? Are you trying to seek attention from men or are you trying to please God? Now, don't get me wrong, I'm not saying having these things are wrong, I'm saying that there's something wrong if you're trying to use them to hide something or to compensate for something that's missing from your life. God loves us too much to let us go on trying to hide our hurts and hang-ups. Either we can lay our mess out before Him, or He will strip it away, baring all our secrets. Laying our lives down before God isn't punishment, although it may feel like it sometimes, it's the first step to freedom. In placing our junk on the altar, our spirit is fighting with our flesh, so there's pain, but it's what frees us. Another verse that really sticks out to me is chapter 4 verse 1. According to the world, there seems to be a timeline for marriage and kids. If you're not married by say, age 30, forget about it, and you can cancel having kids. There's always a time limit, something to push anxiety. God says to be anxious for nothing! (Philippians 4:6) The only timeline you need to worry about is God's. He knows His plans for you (Jeremiah 29:11). Trust Him and stop trying to take matters into your own hand! Just because things don't happen when you want in the way you want doesn't give you the right to go and try to force things to happen especially when it's outside of the will of God. Impatience is what gets so many people in so much trouble! YOU CAN'T FIND A GOOD MAN TO marry you and have kids with so you marry the first somewhat decent man that comes along and all the while you know that he is not the one God has for you but you marry him anyway and end up in the most miserable marriage ever! Or, you decide that you don't want to wait for a man because your biological clock is ticking, and you're getting old, and you want to have babies now, so you go out and get pregnant by some random guy that you claim that you don't need because you're Ms. Independent and don't need a man; but what about that child? You lower your standards just for the sake of saying you have a man, or you're in a marriage that shouldn't have happened in the first place, but you refused to listen to wisdom and you just accept your life of misery. You compromise; yes, you know he's cheating on you but, at least you can say you have someone or that you can say, you're married, yet you wear the pain of disobedience all over your body. You're not fooling anyone, and you're not fooling God. He sees all your junk, and guess what? He's not mad at you, He's hurting for you. Yes, for you. This is why He sent Jesus.

Read the Bible, and stop watching these crappy reality shows! It's not real! Most this mess is scripted! God has so much more for you! Take a moment tonight and strip yourself down and really look at yourself. Get your journal or kneel before God or however or whatever it takes, and lay your junk down. He tells us to cast all our cares on Him because He cares for us (1 Peter 5:6-8). Don't try to cover it up or fix anything, embrace who you are and lay it all at His feet and DON'T PICK IT BACK UP! Leave it there!

So, what is important to God, you ask?

1 Peter 3:3-4 (AMP)

3 Let not yours be the [merely] external adorning with [elaborate] [ ]interweaving and knotting of the hair, the wearing of jewelry, or changes of clothes;
4 But let it be the inward adorning and beauty of the hidden person of the heart, with the incorruptible and unfading charm of a gentle and peaceful spirit, which [is not anxious or wrought up, but] is very precious in the sight of God.

What's inside of you is what's important to God. He looks at our hearts (1 Samuel 16:7). Spend time learning all you can about the Lover of your soul. Read His word and see what He says about you. Then, get rid of what the world says and the negative things that you say about yourself and embrace all that you were created to be. Then, when the time is right, God will bring you to your Adam (Genesis 2:22).

~Thoughts~

Precious Woman of God ♡♡

> GENESIS 2:21-22 (NKJV)
> *21 AND THE LORD GOD CAUSED A DEEP SLEEP TO FALL ON ADAM, AND HE SLEPT, AND HE TOOK ONE OF HIS RIBS, AND CLOSED THE FLESH IN ITS PLACE. 22 THEN THE RIB WHICH THE LORD GOD HAD TAKEN FROM MAN, HE MADE INTO A WOMAN, AND HE BROUGHT HER TO THE MAN.*

I believe that we are God's daughters, His princesses, His babies. When God created woman, He took His time. He put Adam to sleep, so God was fully committed and devoted to the process of designing and creating His daughter as the angels watched in awe. **HE DIDN'T CREATE US FROM THE OPINIONS, THOUGHTS, OR INPUTS FROM MAN.** God created and designed us with the miraculous ability to bring forth life, He created us with great talents and an amazing capacity to love. He gave us beautiful features and precious emotions, fashioned after His own.

THEN, ONCE HE WAS DONE, HE PRESENTED THE WOMAN TO THE MAN AND THE MAN WAS PLEASED WITH WHAT HE SAW. JUST AS GOD CREATED HER NAKED, BEAUTIFUL, AND UNASHAMED. There was no makeup, no weight to be gained or lost, no nipping or tucking. Nothing to change or remove, just total awe and acceptance just as she was given to him, directly from God.

We are a gift created by God, given to man. We should carry and treat ourselves as such. There were no distractions or interruptions, no mistakes when God was creating, molding, and designing us beautiful women. So, don't you dare look at yourself as a mistake, a screw-up, ugly, pitiful charity case who should be glad that you even got a person to look your way! God knew exactly what He was doing, and all these negative thoughts are lies from the pit of hell! You are beautiful, you were fashioned and beautifully designed by the creator of the universe. He stopped all He was doing just to take His sweet time to create us, the beautifully, awesome woman!

~Thoughts~

Change

We all go through changes in our lives, some good, and some bad. Some much needed and some unexpected. Change can bring us such immense joy, or it can feel as if our lives are falling apart as if your heart is being ripped from your chest! Whether we like it or not, change is inevitable.

I remember a period in my life where there was great, dramatic change! I quit my job in 2010 because God said that it was time to go but I thought it was just to leave that job and go to another, but not so! Little did I know God, had something else in store for me, something huge and beyond me. Something that would require my whole life to be changed, shaken and reformed! It didn't feel good at all! BUT, I knew who's in control, and I knew that He had me. If you're a child of God and you have said: "Lord, I surrender my life to you" then hold on for the ride of your life!

Jesus came to die for our sins, so when we surrender our lives to Him, we die to our sins, our plans. That death to our sins is not always easy, but it's necessary for our lives. The change can be painful at times but in the end, it's so good for us, it is life for us. But because we still have flesh, we die kicking and screaming because we don't want to change because change doesn't always feel good. We want what feels good, right? God is more concerned about the development of our character and changing our hearts than our comfort. He said He would never leave nor forsake us, but He never said that this journey would be easy. We all have things about us that we need to change or would like to change, but it's a great relief to know that we don't have to go through the process of change alone. God is patient and gentle with us, gently nudging us in the way we should go. I know sometimes He's probably had to drag me! But out of His great love, He changes us, gently and lovingly. So, if you're in some stuff and you know you shouldn't be or have some things about you that you want to change, don't worry about having to do it all by yourself because you can't, that's why Jesus died for us. We are incapable of this type of change without Jesus. He will help you. All you have to do is ask and obey! He didn't come to condemn but to save and love us. Talk to Him about the things you want to change, need to change but just can't seem to do on your own and trust Him to help you because He will, He's just waiting for the invitation!

~Thoughts~

Crutch

Do you have a crutch? You know, something you go to when you going through a challenging time? Or is it someone? My crutch was food, sugar to be exact. I was an emotional eater. I ate when I was mad, sad, happy, or glad and if there was sugar involved I was even more ecstatic! But the issue in having a crutch is that it doesn't help, it only harms and makes things worse. It's a temporary fix to what's really going on inside. I had to deal with my issues. I couldn't move forward in anything until I did. I had to face my feelings of insecurity, low self-esteem, and lack of self-confidence. The sugar's effects on my body only exacerbated my issues! Every year, my church does a twenty-one day fast, and one year I did the Daniel fast which meant no sugar. The withdrawal from the sugar had me on my knees in my closet crying out to God because I hadn't realized just how strong of a hold that sugar had on me! I depended more on the temporary good feelings from eating sugar than depending on God for help and to fulfill me. God met me where I was. He was loving, and He guided and redirected me. I would say that I have successfully kicked the habit of being an emotional eater! I eat clean, work out a whole lot more than I ever have before, and I pray! I am in constant contact with God, all day, every day. I know my triggers now, and I know to go the opposite direction and to pray and ask God for a way out of the tempting situation.

Now, what's your crutch? What/Who do you depend on to define you? Comfort you? Have you found yourself settling for a guy or relationship that hurts you and hinders you just because it gives a false sense of security? Or do you have the same problem that I had and food has become your savior instead of Jesus? Deep down you know it's not good for you, but you feel that you can't let go? I'm here to tell you that you can. Philippians 4:13 tells us that we can do all things through Christ who strengthens us. Jesus Christ, who rose from the dead, is here to help us with anything that we need. You must understand your need and understand that the thing, situation you want to change is bigger than you and that you can't do it alone. He isn't going to force you to change to do what's best for you. You must want it for yourself. No, it won't be easy but aren't you worth it? Aren't you worthy of true love the way that God designed? Aren't you worthy of health? God wants us to prosper in all things and be in health, just as our soul prospers (3 John 1:2). Nothing worth having will come easy. I go to the gym and kick my own butt, and there are days where my tears mix in with my sweat, but I keep going because I am worth it! So are you! Drop the crutches and walk! God is waiting to bless you with the wonderful life that He had planned for you from the very beginning. Trust Him to catch you when you let go of the crutches, He will never let you fall. After all, He did say that He would never leave or forsake us!

~Thoughts~

Sex

1 Corinthians 6:18 (NKJV)
Flee sexual immorality. Every sin that a man does is outside the body, but he who commits sexual immorality sins against his own body.

5 Things to Think About Before You Have Sex ♥♥

1. Why Am I Doing This or Thinking About Doing This?
- The most important thing you can do is stop and think!
- Am I trying to get him to love me?
- Am I seeking approval?
- Am I trying to prove something?
- Am I trying to fill a void?

2. WHAT AM I TRYING TO GET OUT OF THIS?
- Love?
- Marriage Proposal?
- Kids?
- Security?
- Stability?
- Just an orgasm?

3. WHAT ARE THE CONSEQUENCES?
- Does he have any STD's/STI's, HIV/AIDS?
- Will I get pregnant?
- Will he stick around afterward?
- What happens to my reputation?
- What happens to me emotionally and spiritually?

4. HOW WILL I FEEL AFTERWARDS?
- Hurt?
- Empty?
- Happy?
- Sad?
- Disappointed?
- Fulfilled/Unfulfilled?

5. DO WE REALLY LOVE & KNOW EACH OTHER?
- If you have to question, then you should move no further!

SO, WHY NOT WAIT?

If you both love each other, then wait! Get to know each other more and talk about consequences of having sex, talk about sexual history, set healthy boundaries. Get to know yourself, your likes, dislikes, wants, needs, desires, career, and life goals. Does he know these things about himself? Sex carries a great responsibility. It's not to be taken lightly or casually. It has consequences that you can't dismiss or escape so is it worth rushing into?

~Thoughts~

Overcoming the Desire to Fornicate

Looking back on the days before I surrendered my life to Christ, I think about what was going on in my mind when I gave myself away— gave my body away so freely. It was a result of ignorance, loneliness, seeking acceptance, all of which came from not knowing God and having a personal relationship with Him.

What we see and know about sex from the world's point of view is far removed from God's purpose for it. In the world, sex is used to determine a man's "swag" status, to degrade women and it's used to define us. Many believe if you haven't had sex by a certain age, there must be something wrong with you. The media sends the same message. You're either lame or old fashioned if you're not testing the waters by having sex before marriage.

Sex was designed to be a gift from God to married couples. The act brings closeness. It's sacred. It is intimate. It's a representation of the beautiful covenant relationship that God desires to have with us. When you have sex with someone that is not your spouse, you are creating a soul tie that is difficult to break.

How does one overcome these desires? We overcome through our greatest defense: by being armed with God's Word! John 16:33 (NIV) says "I HAVE TOLD YOU THESE THINGS, SO THAT IN ME YOU MAY HAVE PEACE. IN THIS WORLD, YOU WILL HAVE TROUBLE. BUT TAKE HEART! I HAVE OVERCOME THE WORLD." 1 John 5:4(NIV) says "FOR EVERYONE BORN OF GOD OVERCOMES THE WORLD. THIS IS THE VICTORY THAT HAS OVERCOME THE

WORLD, EVEN OUR FAITH." We have this in us! Our God has OVERCOME this world, and thus we are equipped to overcome the sin of fornication.

Distorting God's purpose for sex is one of Satan's greatest weapons against us. To fight back, we must know God's Word and then exercise our power of standing firm on His word. We stand firmly by:

1. **KNOWING WHO WE ARE IN CHRIST!** "For we are God's workmanship, created in Christ Jesus to do good works, which God prepared in advance for us to do." (Ephesians 2:10 NIV)

2. **PUTTING ON THE FULL ARMOR OF GOD!** "FINALLY, BE STRONG IN THE LORD AND IN HIS MIGHTY POWER. PUT ON THE FULL ARMOR OF GOD SO THAT YOU CAN TAKE YOUR STAND AGAINST THE DEVIL'S SCHEMES. FOR OUR STRUGGLE IS NOT AGAINST FLESH AND BLOOD, BUT AGAINST THE RULERS, AGAINST THE AUTHORITIES, AGAINST THE POWERS OF THIS DARK WORLD AND AGAINST THE SPIRITUAL FORCES OF EVIL IN THE HEAVENLY REALMS." (Ephesians 6:10-11 NIV). Don't be deceived my brothers and sisters, we are in a war for our souls, and you can't go to war unprepared and unprotected!

3. **CHECKING OUR THOUGHTS!** "WE DEMOLISH ARGUMENTS AND EVERY PRETENSION THAT SETS ITSELF UP AGAINST THE KNOWLEDGE OF GOD, AND WE TAKE CAPTIVE EVERY THOUGHT TO MAKE IT OBEDIENT TO CHRIST." (2 Cor. 10:5 NIV). We know that the world is the total opposite of God. Whatever the Word warns us of, the world says, "go for it", "if it feels good do it"! We, children of the Most High God have God's Word to stand on to refute the devil! We also know that "THE WISDOM OF THIS WORLD

IS FOOLISHNESS IN GOD'S SIGHT" (1 Corinthians 3:19 NIV) and if we're not careful, our thoughts can take us for a ride! Instead, we are to think on things that are noble, right, pure, etc. (Philippians 4:8 NIV)

4. **CHECKING THE COMPANY WE KEEP!** Yes, Jesus hung with sinners, but He didn't allow them to cause Him to sin. Instead, He drew them to Him by the way He lived His life. We are to let our light shine! If the company you keep isn't respecting you and your choices to stand on God's Word and keep yourself pure, then you may need to find new friends. "DO NOT BE MISLED: "BAD COMPANY CORRUPTS GOOD CHARACTER" (1 Corinthians 15:33 NIV).

5. **CHECK WHAT WE'RE FEEDING OUR SPIRIT!** What we read, listen to, and watch on TV affects us whether we realize it or not. IN RETURN TO THE GARDEN: EMBRACING GOD'S DESIGN FOR SEXUALITY Kay Arthur writes "WHEN YOU READ HEART, THINK MIND. THE MOST POWERFUL SEX ORGAN IS THE MIND! THE MIND IS STIMULATED PRIMARILY BY WHAT IT SEES." Our worship pastor, Montell Jordan, says "we should ask if what we're listening to is pleasing to the Spirit that lives in us." If what we look at and listen to isn't pleasing to the Spirit then, we shouldn't take it in. (1 Corinthians 3:16-17 NIV).

6. **THINK OF THE END RESULT!** Thinking before you act can keep you from a lifetime of problems. There's no such thing as a "one night stand" as sex has lasting effects. The feelings and connections during and afterward are what bring on the desires. Having sex outside of marriage is selfish. Your body, your virginity is your gift to your spouse, and their gift to you.

That one time can lead to unplanned/unwanted pregnancy, diseases, emotional heartache, and pain, and the scariest one of all, a stronghold on your life for Satan! Think about your future and all the wonderful things that God has planned for you before you decide to give in to your desires.

7. **FORGIVE YOURSELF!** If you've messed up, repent, quickly, dust yourself off and keep pressing on. (Romans 8:1 NIV) says "THAT THERE IS NOW NO CONDEMNATION FOR THOSE WHO ARE IN CHRIST JESUS." Jesus doesn't condemn you, and neither should you condemn yourself!

Hebrews 12:16 (MSG) "WATCH OUT FOR THE ESAU SYNDROME: TRADING AWAY GOD'S LIFELONG GIFT TO SATISFY A SHORT-TERM APPETITE. YOU WELL KNOW HOW ESAU LATER REGRETTED THAT IMPULSIVE ACT AND WANTED GOD'S BLESSING—BUT BY THEN IT WAS TOO LATE, TEARS OR NO TEARS." Yes, our God can restore and redeem but why go through the pain and heartache?

~Thoughts~

Cloudy Vision

Have you ever had cloudy vision? You can see, but not clearly, you can make out shapes and silhouettes but not a clear picture of who or what it is you're looking at? Well, that's what sex before marriage does. Let me explain. You have sex with someone based on how they make you feel or what state of mind you're in. If it's a first-night thing, then you may have sex with the guy for several reasons, you're horny, he's fine, you're lonely, or you feel that you have to just to keep him. Now, say he's not so much of a creep in the beginning, and the sex is good, and all seems fine. Question, what is the basis for this relationship? Is it just sex? We as women have the tendency, just as guys, to "diversify our accounts". We have a guy for sex, for emotional support, who makes us laugh, gives us money, makes us feel good, you name it there's a guy for it! But what about when you decide you're ready to settle down with one guy? You can't marry them all! So now, you're stuck with cloudy vision. You can't make up your mind, the sex guy is cool, but he doesn't give you what you need emotionally, or the emotional guy is cool but you've had sex with him as well, and it wasn't all that hot. So, what do you do?

This used to be me! I wish I'd known that yep, God takes care of that too, and very well. I always say that I got lucky because I married the guy who fit my important needs and as a bonus he's everything I've ever wanted physically. God can take care of our desires as well! *(Psalm 37:4)* My husband's strengths are my weaknesses, and my strengths are his weaknesses. When you have sex with different guys, play the field and get wrapped up in so much mess, you can't see straight, your vision is cloudy! Your heart is jacked up, your emotions are all over the place, and that's

not God's plan for us. He created us, so He knows what we need sexually and emotionally. We don't have to go and do the work by trial and error (mostly error!), He will do it for us gladly.
Jeremiah 29:11-13 says, For I know the plans I have for you declares the Lord, plans to prosper you and not to harm you, plans to give you hope and a future. Then you will call upon me and come and pray to me, and I will listen to you. You will seek me and find me when you seek me with all your heart. See, He's already declared that we're taken care of, but we must have a relationship, not religion with Him and seek Him first! We don't know who we are or what we want or what our purpose is without Him! The way I see it, my life was an absolute mess without God! I tried to do everything on my own and on my own terms and messed up a lot. God loves us so much that He will restore us, pick us up out of our messes and turn them into the beautifulness that He intended for us to have anyway! So, if your vision is cloudy, ask God to give you unclouded vision, and an undivided heart and He will show you the way!

~Thoughts~

Truth & Lies

EPHESIANS 6:14 STAND THEREFORE, HAVING GIRDED YOUR LOINS WITH TRUTH, AND HAVING PUT ON THE BREASTPLATE OF RIGHTEOUSNESS...

This scripture makes me wonder, how many people don't protect their literal "loins" with the truth? How many people really know the truth about sex and how many are listening to the lies of this world? Do you know the truth? Or are you listening to the lies? So below, I've listed a few (although there are many!) of the lies of this world and below that I've listed the truth, from GOD! God, who loves you unconditionally and would never ask you to compromise yourself, or do anything to hurt you, who has great plans for you and wants to protect you! Yes, HIM! Ok, so here we go:

Lies

1. God doesn't care about my sex life.

2. This is my body, and I can do what I want with it!

3. Everyone is having sex. It's no big deal!

4. Oral sex isn't sex.

5. It it's okay for a man to get as much sex as he wants and be single, why can't I?

6. I couldn't help myself!

7. One time won't hurt anything!

8. Nothing will happen, I won't get pregnant, he doesn't have a disease, and he's too cute to have a disease!

9. Not having sex before marriage is old school, no one waits for marriage anymore!

10. It's ok for me to dress like the women I see in music videos, that's what guys like!

Truth

1. God does care very much about our sex life! He created sex! *(1 Thessalonians 4:1-8 NLT)*

2. No, your body does NOT belong to you. Your body is the temple of the Lord! *(1 Corinthians 6:17 NLT)*

3. Everyone may be having sex, but it doesn't mean that it's the right thing to do. It's a huge deal in the eyes of God. He says to flee from sexual immorality. *(1 Corinthians 6:12-18 NLT)*

4. Oral sex is an act of sex, an extension of the gift that God has given to married couples, male & female. *(Song of Songs 2:3, 4:16)*

5. No man or woman, single or not should be having sex with whoever, whenever! God never said to "sow your royal oats", that's from a movie, not God! We are to take pleasure in our HUSBANDS! Not boyfriend, not through hookin' up, and definitely not because you're bored or it's the thing to do! *(Proverbs 5:15-23)*

6. You can't control yourself, but with God's help, you can! *(1 Corinthians 10: 12-13)*

7. One time won't hurt anything…please, all it takes is one time to contract a disease or get pregnant. Sperm was

created to swim, and that's what they are going to do, swim towards the egg and fertilize it! Condoms are not 100%! Your virginity is a one-time gift that's to be for your future husband, trust me, it's worth the wait. There's so much that happens spiritually when you have sex with someone.

8. You can't look at someone and see if they have herpes, HIV/AIDS, syphilis, gonorrhea, etc., and just because a condom is used, it doesn't mean that you're protected. If he has something and his penis touches you anywhere in the area that's supposed to be covered by your panties, there's a chance he's sharing more than just sex with you!

9. There's a reason that God saves sex for marriage. He knows what it was created for and anything outside of why it was created can and will lead to disaster. Think of a can of Drano, if you don't follow the directions on the can, or if you use it for something for which it was NOT created, what do you think will happen? Read the Creator's directions and follow them carefully!

10. The way you dress says a lot about you! How do you want a guy to view you? He will treat you the way that you are dressed. The eyes and mind work hand in hand, and we all know that guys are stimulated greatly by what they see. If you dress like a whore (yeah, I went there!), then, you will be treated like one. There's a way to look attractive without looking like a prostitute. Read the Song of Solomon and see how the man pays attention to every detail of the woman and tells her how beautiful she is, shoot, he even talks about her teeth! Every woman wants to be loved, treasured, and appreciated, so make sure you're giving him a reason to love, treasure and appreciate you for who you

are and not just the way your butt looks or how big your breasts are. Those are for your husband's enjoyment only!

There's so much more on this subject but please, get a Bible, or better yet, go on the internet to an online Bible and find a version that makes sense to you and learn the truth for yourself. Don't listen to your friends, TV, or the radio. Read the Bible for yourself and get the truth for yourself. God has a plan for all of us, and it's a great plan! It's not for us to be hurt and defeated but to prosper and have an abundant and full life. You don't have to settle for the lies of this world!

~Thoughts~

Facing Truth ♡

Sometimes facing the truth about ourselves can be extremely hard! It's hard facing the ugliness that's within us. The impure thoughts and feelings, pride. Our actions that oftentimes come from selfishness and us wanting our own way. But the Word of God says that the truth shall set us free *(John 8:32)*, so why wouldn't we want to face the truth? Don't we all want to be free? Jesus paid the price for our freedom, all we need to do is face the truth and repent. It's painful at first, I won't discount that, but the act of looking inward and confessing truly is freeing.

What's the truth you ask? The truth is that we're all sinners. None of us have it all together and we never will as long as we're on this earth (I don't know about you, but this revelation alone gives me peace!). But, with Jesus and His truth, we can have peace, unconditional love, joy, mercy, grace, and freedom. His freedom from our sins and all the things on the inside of us that hurts us and holds us in bondage, we must face it, confess it, repent, and move forward in the freedom of Christ!

Facing the truth of our sins is painful. You must stop and think about what you're doing and why you're doing it. The why is the most painful I think. For me, facing my sexual sin was the most painful because of the reasons I was having sex outside of marriage. I was trying to escape my life. I was trying to find love and solace amid my chaotic, dysfunctional life. I needed an escape from my mom's drug and alcohol addiction, from my sister's rebelliousness, from the pain of not fitting in. I needed an escape and sex was it. It was supposed salve to my broken heart. It was all I knew because I didn't know that God loved me and was willing and ready to take away my pain. I was never taught that; all I knew was what I saw. It was either drugs or sex, and I wasn't turning to drugs! Sex provided a false sense of security that I thought would bring me all that I needed to end my pain, but it only added to my pain. Sin never heals or helps, it makes things worse. The wages of sin is death! *(Romans 6:23)* Nothing good ever comes from sin. I know that saving sex for marriage, being a virgin isn't the most popular thing in the world but look at the consequences of the alternative. How many young girls are pregnant and responsible for a child and never really had a chance to be a child themselves? How many are living with sexually transmitted diseases? How many are seeking sex for love but in the end, are hurt each and every time? We have no business having sex outside of marriage! That's not what God, the creator of sex, intended. Sex is for marriage, a mature act that should only happen between married couples. There's a spiritual deepness, a connection that happens when you have sex with someone, which is why it shouldn't be had outside the covenant of marriage.

Once you have sex, everything about you changes. Facing the truth about ourselves, our situations, whatever the case may be, is not always pleasant but it's always necessary and needed, and it brings freedom. Peace comes from facing the truth and letting all the lies go. Peace comes from Jesus Christ, surrendering our lives to Him. He came to give us peace! *(John 14:27)*. Don't be afraid to face your past or your present, your future truly depends on it. Jesus is always here waiting to love, not condemn us. *(Romans 8:1-2)*.

~Thoughts~

Temptation is a Beast!

Genesis 3:1-6
*1 Now the serpent was more crafty than any of the wild animals the Lord God had made. He said to the woman, "**Did God really say,** 'You must not eat from any tree in the garden'?"*
2 The woman said to the serpent, "We may eat fruit from the trees in the garden, 3 but God did say, 'You must not eat fruit from the tree that is in the middle of the garden, and you must not touch it, or you will die.'"
4 "You will not certainly die," the serpent said to the woman.5 "For God knows that when you eat from it, your eyes will be opened, and you will be like God, knowing good and evil."
6 When the woman saw that the fruit of the tree was good for food and pleasing to the eye, and also desirable for gaining wisdom, she took some and ate it. She also gave some to her husband, who was with her, and he ate it.

I know we've all been in situations where we've wanted to do something so badly, and we tried to rationalize or come up with a way to justify our reasoning for doing what we shouldn't do or did. Well, this is where Eve is. The serpent broke her down by providing reasons that eating the fruit was good and beneficial to both her and her husband. Isn't this the case when we're tempted? All the stupid things we think of start to sound so smart and fool proof. Satan's strategy is to confuse reality and make you doubt God and yourself.

Here's the Scene: You're with this guy, he looks good, smells good, sounds good, and he must be good, right? So, you guys are connecting, and there's so much chemistry between you two it could cause an explosion! Then he starts pleading his case, I won't tell anyone, it will be just between you and me, I won't hurt you, leave you, blah, blah, blah! So, what are you going to do? What's the worst that could happen? Can you trust him? Your hormones are in such an uproar you can't even think straight! Well, this is what you do...RUN! Take off the heels and RUN! The Bible says to flee from sexual immorality! Not walk away, keep in touch, email, text, sit next to, no, RUN, FLEE! *(1 Corinthians 6:18).*

The first step to handling temptation is not putting yourself in a situation where you are alone with a guy! Especially if you're attracted to each other. Go out in groups and make sure that there is someone in the group who will hold you accountable for your actions, who will remind you of all the things you can't seem to think of when Mr. Fineness is around! Remember, temptation is a beast! Don't think you can fool it or outsmart it. There's always a way out, God will always provide one so be on the lookout for it if you're ever in a tempting situation.

1 Corinthians 10:12-13
12 So, if you think you are standing firm, be careful that you don't fall! 13 No temptation has overtaken you except what is common to mankind. And God is faithful; he will not let you be tempted beyond what you can bear. But when you are tempted he will also provide a way out so that you can endure it.

~Thoughts~

Scriptures for When You're Being Tempted

A wise woman of God will think ahead to the consequences of giving in to the temptations that she might be faced with. What would happen to us if we compromised our morals? How would we feel if we gave in to the temptations? Who would our consequences affect? How would the consequences affect our family members, our spouse, and friends? There's no way we can fight temptations without the Holy Spirit as our guide and without knowing God's word. So, here are a few scriptures to arm you with:

Ephesians 6:10-18 (NLT)

10 A final word: Be strong in the Lord and in his mighty power. 11 Put on all of God's armor so that you will be able to stand firm against all strategies of the devil. 12 For we[·] are not fighting against flesh-and-blood enemies, but against evil rulers and authorities of the unseen world, against mighty powers in this dark world, and against evil spirits in the heavenly places.

13 Therefore, put on every piece of God's armor, so you will be able to resist the enemy in the time of evil. Then after the battle, you will still be standing firm. 14 Stand your ground, putting on the belt of truth and the body armor of God's righteousness. 15 For shoes, put on the peace that comes from the Good News so that you will be fully prepared.[·] 16 In addition to all of these, hold up the shield of faith to stop the fiery arrows of the devil.[·] 17 Put on salvation as your helmet, and take the sword of the Spirit, which is the word of God.
18 Pray in the Spirit at all times and on every occasion. Stay alert and be persistent in your prayers for all believers everywhere.

Matthew 26:41 (NLT)

41 Keep watch and pray, so that you will not give in to temptation. For the spirit is willing, but the body is weak!"

James 1:12-18 (NLT)

12 God blesses those who patiently endure testing and temptation. Afterward, they will receive the crown of life that God has promised to those who love him. 13 And remember, when you are being tempted, do not say, "God is tempting me." God is never tempted to do wrong, [a] and he never tempts anyone else. 14 Temptation comes from our own desires, which entice us and drag us away. 15 These desires give birth to sinful actions. And when sin is allowed to grow, it gives birth to death.
16 So don't be misled, my dear brothers and sisters. 17 Whatever is good and perfect comes down to us from God our Father, who created all the lights in the heavens.[a] He never changes or casts a shifting shadow.[a] 18 He chose to give birth to us by giving us his true word. And we, out of all creation, became his prized possession.

Galatians 6:1 (NLT)

6 Dear brothers and sisters, if another believer[a] is overcome by some sin, you who are godly[b] should gently and humbly help that person back onto the right path. And be careful not to fall into the same temptation yourself.

~Thoughts~

How to Say No

In the October 2011 edition of Essence magazine is an article all the way in the back of the magazine called *"Our Teens' Secret Sex Lives"*. I'm ticked that the article wasn't mentioned on the front page! This is a serious issue. I read the article when I was in a bookstore and I wanted to just break down and cry! Not that I expected to see any mention of God and His truths about sex in the article but reading this article just stabbed my heart with the fact that God is being removed from everything to please those who don't believe and the only way to eradicate premarital/premature sex is through God! His word will tell you everything you need to know about sex! If you don't have a relationship with God (notice I said relationship and NOT religion), then you will be lost and hurt by the lies and evils of this world.

They interviewed this one girl who was 14 years old (I was 14 the first time I had sex), and she said that she was frustrated at the **way** her mom was telling her not to have sex and telling her to wait 3 months to even let a boy kiss you! The young girl admits that at her school they're not even in a relationship with a guy that long! She wants to know why guys are so pushy and to sum it all up, **she wants to know how to say no!**

I was shocked! As parents, (yep I'm included!) when we're approached with something we don't want to talk about or explain or don't know how to explain, we say "because I said so!" Well, guess what? That doesn't work! We must be honest, open, and transparent about our lives and what happened to us! They want and need to know why you say no, and if you don't tell them then guess where they're going to find their answers? I wish my mom had told me about her life, the bad and ugly, not just the good.

So, to all the young girls and single women who find themselves in compromised situations here are a few suggestions on how to say no:

1. **Pray & Run!** If you're in a situation, pray that God will show you the way out and flee! (See the section on Temptation!)
2. **Cherish, respect and treasure yourself!** If a guy promises you forever, ask him to spell it and show you by marrying you! No lip service, action please! Don't just give yourself to some dude because he looks good, smells good and sounds good. You're worth much more than that! God paid a high price for you so act the part. He didn't send Jesus for nothing!
3. **Never ever go out on a date alone! Never ever find yourself alone with a guy/man that you're attracted to or who is attracted to you!**
4. **Check your friends.** Do you all share the same beliefs and morals? Is she going to hold you accountable for your actions? Look out for you and let you know when you're thinking of doing something you'll regret later? As women, we need that!

If you follow these, you won't have to worry about compromising your body, your beliefs, or your morals. **Please remember that everything you do now affects your future!**

~Thoughts~

Triggers

Walking in purity isn't easy, whether you're married or not. Yes, married folks must check themselves on purity as well! Being married doesn't get you out of the walking in purity thing. I'm not just speaking of sexual purity but purity in our minds and hearts as well. We all have certain triggers. We are emotional, feeling individuals and the way we process things are by using our five senses. By using these five senses, we find that there are certain triggers that either excite our senses or they don't. Knowing those triggers plays an important part to walking in purity.

One of the most important things in walking in purity is knowing and accepting that you CANNOT do it alone. You need Jesus Christ, point, blank, period! Jesus was tempted himself by Satan *(Matthew 4:1),* so He understands that we will be tempted but He doesn't allow us to be tempted beyond what we can bear and He provides a way out for us *(1 Corinthians 10:13)*. Notice, He as in Jesus, not us. We can't save ourselves, we can't help ourselves, and we can't overcome sin in our own strength, that's why Jesus died for us on the Cross. Apart from Him, we can do nothing *(John 15:5)*. If you have decided that you're going to live a life of purity and you're trying to do it without Him, good luck!

Now, back to triggers. The world is full of triggers that the enemy has set to trip us up, and I'm going to give you a little list of them to be aware of:

1. People: Yes, people. You know that one guy (or several) who looks at you a certain way, smells so good, has muscles, and walks a certain way that gets you all hot and bothered? Or the one who's always checking on you and just the sound of his voice gets you to smile so big that all your pearly whites are showing? Yes, him, run from him! Divert your eyes, keep your hands to yourself, hold your breath when he walks by or just look at his shoes when he walks by (this is what I used to do). Do whatever it takes to be successful and pray. Also, other people you should avoid are those who don't share the same moral values as you do. You need to be around people who are going to hold you accountable, not assist you in falling!

2. *Music:* What are you listening to? I can't even bear to listen to some of the crap that's on the radio now! Everything is talking about sex, no wonder so many people fall! What are you feeding yourself? If you keep listening to what Chris Brown, Trey Songz, and whoever else wants to do in the bedroom, guess what, you're going to want to find out. Never underestimate the power of music. For instance, when you're feeling sad, there are songs we listen to help us feel better, when we exercise there are certain songs we listen to get us pumped up and ready to go, well there's music that makes you want to do stuff you have no business doing outside of marriage, and there are songs that promote violence as well. Why does music have so much power? I'll give you a brief Bible lesson. Satan, before he was kicked out of Heaven, used to be Lucifer, the archangel of worship, music. So now that he's been made a prince of this world, just like sex, he's also perverted the use of music. So now instead of all music glorifying God, there's music that now glorifies Satan. Satan wants glory, and God is the only one who gets glory, which is one of the reasons Satan was kicked out. So, music is one of his weapons. If what you're listening to isn't encouraging you or glorifying God, don't listen to it! Period! I understand about the "tight beats" but that's how the enemy sucks you in! Tight beat or not, if the words are not glorifying God, move along.

3. Television: Oh, my goodness, I don't know where to start other than just saying stick to HGTV and Food Network. I'll give it to you this way, your eyes are the window to your soul. What are you allowing in? If you want a godly relationship, why are you watching shows like Scandal? TV, just like music, affects our mood and our emotions. Be mindful of what you watch. The crap they show on TV is scripted, planned. They have all kinds of tricks that they use to make people and situations look so good, but it's all a lie! The Bible says in Jeremiah 29:11 that God has great plans for us, it's already been written, trust God's script for your life, you'll never be disappointed!

4. Media: Facebook, Twitter, Instagram, etc. can be blessings or curses. If I were to look at your FB page, what would I see? Better yet, God sees your FB page, what is He seeing? Did you know that employers use social media to check out potential employees? If it's not positive, encouraging or glorifying God, get rid of it or them! Also, what are you reading? *50 Shades of Grey*? Did you know that our minds are our greatest sex organ? So, if you're reading stuff like this, what's going on in your mind? This is what leads to masturbation. The act of self-gratification. Masturbation is a cop out, and it grieves the Holy Spirit who lives in you. The Bible says to take every thought captive and bring it into obedience to God. *(2 Corinthians 10:5)* What I hate about TV and so-called reality television show is that they are so deceptive. When you get married, you already go in with so many preconceived notions, most of which are wrong and crap like this just adds fuel to the fire. Again, if it's not encouraging or glorifying God, don't read it. Keep your thoughts pure, keep your heart pure.

The best defense against all the mess in this world is the Word of God. Spend time reading the Bible. There's really no excuse now. There are apps galore, free internet sites, the Bible is everywhere, but you must make a choice to make time to read it. If you want to know how to walk a life of purity, start with the Truth. The Truth shall set you free! *(John 8:32)*

~Thoughts~

Self-Control

Proverbs 25:28 (MSG)
28 A person without self-control
is like a house with its doors and windows knocked out.

Proverbs 25:28 (NLT)
28 A person without self-control
is like a city with broken-down walls.

I have this daily devotional book called THE DAILY GOD BOOK: A YEAR OF LISTENING FOR GOD BY ERIN KEELEY MARSHALL and there was a section on Self Control that really made me think. When I think of self-control, I often think of the lack of self-control that I see in the world we live in today. Self-control seems to be extinct in a world whose mantra is "if it feels good, do it". My self-control wanes when it comes to sweets, sugar. I'm a sucker for cupcakes and Ben & Jerry's Coffee Heathbar Crunch! What makes you lose control? Better yet, what environment or situation are you in when you feel your self-control disappearing? Are you in a place where "the doors and windows are knocked out" or your "walls are broken down"? I truly feel this plays a huge part in being successful at keeping ourselves together. If I avoid the cupcake shop and not go to Publix when they have Ben & Jerry's on sale buy one, get one free, then I'm successful at not packing on a few extra pounds and consuming enormous quantities of sugar! Now, if your weakness is something that can truly alter the course of your life, such as sex before marriage, then I suggest you really chew on, ponder, and soak this in. Here are some key points to ponder that I wrote down from this devotional:

1. *A controlling personality isn't regarded as virtuous unless it applies to self-control and God doesn't tell us to do things in His word without giving us the ability to obey Him.*
2. *When God issues commands through Proverbs, He sees us as fully capable of following through on them. This rules out our weak excuse that we can't do it. It's not that we can't, it's that we don't want to!*
3. *Self-control blesses us! It works as a hedge of protection around us in the same way that walls protected cities in Solomon's day.*
4. *Without self-control, we're vulnerable to bad judgment calls, to temptations and to misguided priorities.*
5. *What lies in our power to do, it lies in our power not to do.*

I understand that we're bombarded on an insanely consistent manner about letting loose, but God calls us to a higher standard. Things are only going to get worse, just in case you haven't been reading your Bible. We're going to need God more than ever, and in ways we never thought we would. Strengthen yourself with the Word of God. His Word builds us up and helps us to keep going and helps us to maintain control in a seemingly uncontrollable world. Hold on, you can do it!

~Thoughts~

Cravings

I've been trying to deal with my addiction to sugar for years. I crave it and all things sweet! Sigh… Anyway, sugar, if not taken in moderately can cause many problems in our bodies. So, what in the world do cravings have to do with sex? Well, I'm glad you asked! Your body will crave what you give it! If you consume certain foods or drinks, that's what your body will crave. So, likewise, if you have sex, especially forbidden sex, which is the best according to our flesh, then my friends that's what you'll crave. If you're feeding yourself the things of this world, listening to degrading, sex-infused music, movies with all things sexual, friends who tell of their sexual conquests and suggest you do the same, then your body will start to crave those things. I've been there! Be mindful of what you're feeding yourself. Make sure you're feeding yourself great, life-giving, encouraging things. Make sure you're surrounding yourself with people who will hold you accountable to your standards and morals. You have a choice of what you crave!

~Thoughts~

Pleasing Self

Say that you're single, you've given your life to God and you've decided that you've had enough of the dating scene and you're tired of giving up your goods because it only ends in heartache. You've found ways and "things" to help curb your sexual urges and appetite, so you're good now, right? You don't have to teach anyone how to please you, you don't have to worry about getting pregnant, getting a disease or being disappointed sexually! This is awesome! I don't need a man I'm good with_____! You fill in the blank. Well, you're wrong!

1 Corinthians 6:18 Run from sexual sin! No other sin so clearly affects the body as this one does. For sexual immorality is a sin against your own body.

Masturbation is not your way out. Think of it, does pleasing yourself please God? He's the one that we are here to please, right? Instead of trusting Him to help you deal with your urges and helping you to remain pure until you're married (if it's His will for you to marry) you decide to take matters into your own hands (literally). God's goal for us is to be pure and holy whether we are single or married. Married women, if your husband does not know how to please you sexually, teach him! You're in this together forever! Don't invite anyone else in, don't use "something" to replace him, teach him! Single women, ok, I know it's tough, I've been there, but I didn't have anyone to tell me that God will help me to stay pure! He wants us to remain pure so that we can fully enjoy the wedding gift, sex with our husbands, the way He intended!

When you masturbate, it seems that you have found the right combination of positions, toys, sounds, smells, and thoughts, whatever to help bring you to orgasm. Well, think about this, what if, when you get married, your hubby may be a different size or shape, he may not like a certain position, smell, or even toys, then what? You have an issue, and the last issues you want in marriage are sexual issues! Satan will have a grand old time with this! He's already ticked that you're married, so he's looking for a way to destroy your marriage. Well, by you conditioning your body to climax a certain way and your hubby not being able to bring you to orgasm, well there's Satan's way right there to turn your marriage into a living hell!

Don't despair! There's hope! Remember, God always provides a way out. Well, how in the world does He provide a way for me to deal with this "backlog" of love? God is faithful when He said He would provide a way, He wasn't lying. He can't lie, He's God. He will supply ALL YOUR NEEDS!

Galatians 5:16 So I say, let the Holy Spirit guide your lives. Then you won't be doing what your sinful nature craves.

Sex of any kind outside of marriage indicates a lack of trust in God. You don't trust God to provide for you mentally, emotionally, physically, or sexually. He knows we have needs and urges, that's why He says not to "awaken love until it's time." *(Song of Songs 2:7)* Some women say they need to "try the guy out" to make sure that he's a good fit but I say this, if God created us all then don't you think He knows what it will take to please you sexually? God created sex as well, remember? Trust God to care for you in all ways until you're married. He knows all that you're dealing with and going through. Pray and ask Him to help you with (or remove) your urges until you're married. He will!

~Thoughts~

How will I know?

I saw this on a meme once:

> *"No sex before marriage? Um, excuse me please, but do you buy a car without a test drive?"*
> *Really?! You're going to compare yourself to a car?*

You're a human being, not a frickin' car! Anyway, it doesn't stop people from asking the question though, so I'm going to answer it. In short, you will know by trusting God. Need more? Well, here goes:

God created us in His image: male and female. *(Genesis 1:27)* He knows all about how the bodies are to fit together. He knows the shape and size of each penis He's ever created, and He knows all about each vagina He's ever shaped and formed. He knows how we think, what we think and all our ways. *(Psalms 139:1-4)* He knows us better than we know ourselves. God also knows about sex, after all He created it, which means He also knows why He created it! Sex was created for marriage, and the very first sex act was between Adam and Eve, husband and wife. *(Genesis 4:1)* Even more so, God created Eve without the help, opinions, or input from Adam, he was asleep *(Genesis 2:21)*. Once God was finished creating Eve, He brought Eve to Adam. *(Genesis 2:22)* Now, once Eve was presented to Adam by God, Adam fully accepted her as his wife, bone of his bones, and flesh of his flesh. *(Genesis 2:23)* Note, when Eve was presented to Adam, Adam didn't say to God, "God let me take her for a test drive to make sure she can satisfy me sexually. Let me make sure she is right for me because if she isn't then you're going to have to try again!" No!! Adam trusted

God, Adam trusted the fact that God had made a helper suitable for him in EVERY way! *(Genesis 2:20b* emphasis mine)

If you place all your trust in God, you won't have to give yourself over to guy after guy, tying your soul with them, being hurt by them and each time, giving away a piece of yourself! This is NOT GOD's WAY!! You are not to be test driven like a car! You are the daughter of a King! He wants to give you the desires of your heart, but you must put your trust and faith in Him and WAIT! God is still molding and shaping you into an awesome wife for one of His son's one day, and He doesn't need man's approval! The man that God presents you with will have His stamp of approval, and you can guarantee that God will make sure that His daughter will be satisfied! You will be satisfied and so will your future Hubby. You can't go wrong doing things God's way. He has all the bases covered. He will give you exactly what you need, but you must trust Him.

~Thoughts~

Nothing New Under the Sun!

I was watching an episode of *The Golden Girls* one night that just really ticked me off! In this episode, Rose had been dating this guy for a month and "no action". Nothing, he's made no attempts at sex, and it was kind of bothering her. So, they go away for a weekend, and Rose is hoping things will change in their relationship, but while they're away on their romantic weekend, he tells her that he's impotent. Say what?! She tells him that she's ok with it and they move along in their relationship. Well, all this changes when they go out to dinner and Rose says that she thinks that people put too much emphasis on sex in a relationship and then they both proceed to list all the cons of sex and instead of deterring the issue, she and her boyfriend get all hot and bothered and low and behold, they finally have sex!

Well, Rose is over the moon, and she talks about how much she **LIKES OR MIGHT EVEN LOVE HIM (REALLY?),** and they go on a picnic, only for him to dump her in the end. He thanks her for her patience and for "helping him with his problem" and that he was going to go back to his ex-wife and see if they can work things out because his problem was fixed! Rose said she understood! What the what?! Ok, I know it's only a TV show, and it's from almost 20yrs ago, but nothing's changed! Women fall into this same trap every day! You give up your body and then on to the next as if nothing happened! This guy just totally dismissed Rose! No consideration for her feelings at all!

See how desensitized we've become? Of course, when I watched this when I was little I didn't know what was going on, but now that I do, I think of all the people who've watched this show over the years and have laughed at the constant sexual innuendos, laughed at Blanche's insatiable desire for men and sex and this show just made it all seem like a normal, healthy, funny part of life! All the while, the enemy is rejoicing at how many women are led astray, how many are deceived into thinking that sleeping around, giving your body away is the thing to do!

Ladies, keep your legs closed and your eyes and ears open! LET GOD DO THE MATCHMAKING! Even though this was a TV show, this stuff's going on today, and the ages are much younger. **YOU CAN'T MAKE SOMEONE LOVE YOU BY HAVING SEX WITH THEM!** You don't have to see if you're a perfect match sexually, that's God's job as well. He created you, and He knows what your "needs and desires" are. Love and marriage first. It's not the old-fashioned way, it's God's way, and it's His way for a reason!

Value yourself! You are a DAUGHTER OF THE KING, THE MOST HIGH GOD! You're worth dying for, not just a one night fling with some guy who doesn't care about you! YOU ARE WORTH MORE!

~Thoughts~

Reward?

Ecclesiastes 9:9 (NLT) Live happily with the woman you love through all the meaningless days of life that God has given you under the sun. <u>The wife God gives you is your reward for all your earthly toil.</u>

I was having my quiet time with God, and I read the verse above. I sat and thought, oh wow, I'm my hubby's reward! I never thought of being a wife in this way! I knew that I was a good thing because God's Word says that he who finds a wife finds a good thing, but a reward? Sweet! Then, as I should expect, Holy Spirit, doing what He's supposed to do asks me, so do you think you've been a reward to your husband? Hmm… ouch! I started with "I try, but you know sometimes Lord he does this and says that and he didn't do XYZ." Yeah, then I'm stopped in my extensive list of "but Gods" and am asked again…conviction!

Wow, have I been a reward to my hot hunk of chocolate? Does he see me as his reward for all his hard work and earthly toil? And I had to really check myself, it depends on what day you ask him! Seriously! Does he see me as his reward in the way I dress, my actions, my tone of voice when I speak to him, in taking care of his domestic needs and his sexual needs? Y'all if I really look at myself honestly, I have some work to do!

My married ladies, take some time to look at yourselves. Do you think of yourself as a reward to your husband? Does he see you as his reward? Or, like me, you have some work to do? Our bodies are not our own *(1 Corinthians 7:4)*. I know he ticked you off, and the kids are driving you crazy but remember sex is God's wedding gift to married couples, and God takes pleasure in our pleasure *(Ecclesiastes 9:7 MSG)*.

Single ladies, there will be some days that the man you marry will get on your last nerve, say, or do something that will hurt your feelings but in marriage, we as wives still must do our part regardless of what our hubbies do. *(See 1 Peter 3:1-6 & Ephesians 5:22-24, 33)* It's not always easy, I'll be the first to admit it, but God holds us accountable for our actions according to what He has told us to do. Think of where you are now, would any man see you as his reward or are you giving away your "rewards" to anyone who will take them? After taking a deeper look at your past and divulging your past to your future hubby, would he see you as his reward? There are several reasons God reserves sex for marriage. What you do now affects your future!

~Thoughts~

Giving Up Rights

GENESIS 25:29-34 THE STORY OF JACOB & ESAU

29 ONE DAY JACOB WAS COOKING A STEW. ESAU CAME IN FROM THE FIELD, STARVED.
*You go out on a date with this guy. You're both attracted to each other. You're touching and laughing. He smells and looks good, and so do you! All is going well. In all of this, hormones are stirring up because you are attracted to each other. Ladies, we have chemistry!

30 ESAU SAID TO JACOB, "GIVE ME SOME OF THAT RED STEW-I'M STARVED!" THAT'S HOW HE CAME TO BE CALLED EDOM (RED).
31 JACOB SAID, "MAKE ME A TRADE: MY STEW FOR YOUR RIGHTS AS THE FIRSTBORN."
*When you have sex for the first time with someone who is not your husband, you're giving away, trading your would-be husband's rights (to be your first) to your virginity. You've taken away his gift of being your first, one and only lover.

32 ESAU SAID, "I'M STARVING! WHAT GOOD IS A BIRTHRIGHT IF I'M DEAD?"
*I gotta have you now! I'm horny! I'm going to go crazy if I don't or why do we have to wait? We're here now. One time won't hurt anything; just wanna see if you'll like it or if I'll like you or if we fit together. I won't hurt you; just wanna make you feel good. Any of these sound familiar? Feel free to add to the list!

33 JACOB SAID, "FIRST, SWEAR TO ME." AND HE DID IT. ON OATH, ESAU TRADED AWAY HIS RIGHTS AS THE FIRSTBORN.
*You tell him your fears that he'll leave you, hurt you, get you pregnant and he says no, none of these things will happen. You're convinced and persuaded, and then you give in, you trade away; give away your precious body, your precious gift. You connect with this guy mentally, physically, spiritually, and emotionally – all by having sex with him.

34 JACOB GAVE HIM BREAD AND THE STEW OF LENTILS. HE ATE AND DRANK, GOT UP AND LEFT. THAT'S HOW ESAU SHRUGGED OFF HIS RIGHTS AS THE FIRSTBORN.
*You had sex with him, opened yourself up to him, and then he leaves. You're left wondering if you'll ever hear from him again, will he tell everyone he knows or if perhaps you didn't use protection or the condom broke, you're left wondering did I catch anything from him, is there a chance that I could have gotten pregnant?

In this story, Jacob wanted all the rights that come along with being the first-born child. But they belonged to Esau. But we see in this story that the birthrights don't seem to mean that much to Esau because he gave them away so easily. It says in verse 34 that he shrugged them off. In the dictionary to shrug off means to disregard, minimize, to rid one of. So, when you think of it, when you have sex for the first time with someone who's not your husband, you disregard, make light of and get rid of your gift of virginity, your husband's "birthright" and your beautiful body that God has given you. In the end, you minimize or make yourself look and feel small because you have given in. The reality is that in some cases ignorance plays the greatest part because, just like me, you weren't taught the meaning of sex or what it's all about and that it's more than just not getting pregnant and not contracting a sexually transmitted disease. The intended purpose of sex is to allow a man and woman to unite emotionally and physically, as husband and wife, with the possibility of forming a new human life and becoming parents. Sex is intended to be pleasurable for both the husband and wife. When used for any other purpose, it can result in regret, insecurity, heartache, divorce, abortion, disease, and infection.

When you think about sex, what's the first thing that comes to mind? For me, it was what I'd seen on TV; some fabrications of this couple all hot and heavy going at it as if their lives depended on it. This is awesome if you're married! But for the record, even when you're married, this scene is not always the case! Just saying this, so you will know that TV hypes up everything. That's how the money is made!

Sex was designed and created by God for both pleasure and procreation. Hence "be fruitful and multiply". Sex was given to **MARRIED COUPLES** as a gift. Yes, that's right, a gift! It's a representation of our relationship with God or the relationship He longs to have with us. When you have sex with someone, you become "one" with them. God wants us to become "one" with Him in body and spirit.

Webster's Dictionary defines gift as something freely given; a natural ability. God has freely given us these natural feelings and abilities to experience this wonderful gift for becoming one with our spouse. Yes, it's also a natural ability; it's natural that you will have sexual desires; after all, He gave them to us as well. However, we are warned about awakening these sexual desires in the Bible. Sex is a deep act of love that cannot be expressed by words. Sex is the act that transforms a marriage to a deeper level. It produces intimacy in a way that no other act can. Sex is a universally spoken language of love and one of the most exploited of all our sinful weaknesses. God gave us sex because He wanted us to experience and to have pleasure in our lives. He only wants wonderful things for us! He reserved sex for marriage because he knew the consequences and pain of not doing so. 1 CORINTHIANS 6:12A SAYS THAT "EVERYTHING IS PERMISSIBLE FOR ME: – BUT NOT EVERYTHING IS BENEFICIAL. God gave us free will, but it doesn't give us the right to abuse it. By choosing to have sex outside of marriage, what are you expecting to get out of it? What's the real benefit? Really, sit down and think about it, what are you really getting out of this, 1-5 minutes (maybe!) of pleasure (if it's your first time, pain), then what?

Sexual immorality or fornication is sex outside of marriage or sexual intercourse between unmarried persons. It is a great sin. It is so because when you have sex with someone who you're not married to; you sin against your own body as well as God. 1 CORINTHIANS 6:13-16 SAYS, "THE BODY IS NOT MEANT FOR SEXUAL IMMORALITY, BUT FOR THE LORD, AND THE LORD FOR THE BODY. BY HIS POWER, GOD RAISED THE LORD FROM THE DEAD, AND HE WILL RAISE US ALSO. DO YOU NOT KNOW THAT YOUR BODIES ARE MEMBERS OF CHRIST HIMSELF? SHALL I THEN TAKE THE MEMBERS OF CHRIST AND UNITE THEM WITH A PROSTITUTE? NEVER! DO YOU NOT KNOW THAT HE WHO UNITES HIMSELF WITH A PROSTITUTE IS ONE WITH HER IN BODY? FOR IT IS SAID, "THE TWO WILL BECOME ONE FLESH." BUT HE WHO UNITES HIMSELF WITH THE LORD IS ONE WITH HIM IN SPIRIT. FLEE FROM SEXUAL IMMORALITY. ALL OTHER SINS A MAN

COMMITS ARE OUTSIDE HIS BODY, BUT HE WHO SINS SEXUALLY SINS AGAINST HIS OWN BODY. I never knew this until I gave my life to Christ, until I started reading His Word. A prostitute, seriously?! If you think of it, sex outside of marriage is like prostitution. You give your body away to someone you probably don't intend to marry, and you pay for it, with your body, your life, and your emotional and spiritual self. You're worth more than that!

If you're thinking of having sex outside of marriage, consider this, you're giving away one of the greatest gifts that God has given you. You can't get it back! Also, think about the person you're giving yourself away to. Is he worth it? If so, why not get married first? If you're not ready for marriage, then you're not ready for sex.

~Thoughts~

What did you do?

You ever been in a tempting situation, knew you should run and get out, turn away, but didn't? You think that it's only once or it's just you and all will be well if you give in just this one time?
What happens when you give in? How do you feel afterward? Did your decision only affect you?

Oftentimes when facing tempting situations, we know what we SHOULD do, but we often go with what we WANT TO DO. Never mind who it hurts or the fact that it can hurt us as well. What we fail to realize is that our actions are not just about us, it's about all who are in our lives as well.

As I think about temptations I've faced; feeding into compliments from other guys, eating food that's not good for me, especially sugar, saying things that will hurt instead of edify, not praying, I have to take a minute to pause and think of how giving in will affect others around me and not only that, affect the way that people view me. Some days fighting against our fleshly desires can be extremely hard. I totally get that. If I give in to the compliments and flirt back, what does that say about me, my marriage, and my relationship with God? If I give in to the foods that are not good for me, it will affect my health which affects my family because I won't be able to take care of them if I'm sick. If I "tell it like it is and say what's on my mind", who is it really helping if my words are only hurting the person who's probably only lashing out because they're in pain?

We are warned by our Father against giving in to sin, and we just don't take the time to stop and listen for His direction. Then, we act all hurt and surprised when our consequences hurt us. Then to make matters even worse, we expect God to bless us even though we disobeyed Him! I've been guilty of this. I had to just really think, seriously, why would God bless me for blatantly disobeying Him? What does that say about my view, love and respect for Him?

I know we live in a fast-paced, crazy world, but God still rules and reigns in this madness, and He's still with us and looking out for us amid it all, but it's up to us to stop and listen. God has given us freedom of choice, in Him there is freedom, but He says to not use this freedom to indulge the sinful nature *(Galatians 5:13)*. He says to live by the Spirit, and you will not gratify the desires of the sinful nature. The sinful nature totally contradicts and conflicts with His Spirit *(Galatians 5:16-17)*.

So, the next time you're faced with a tempting situation, stop and listen and think about what you're doing. If you give in, who are you hurting? Want to know the magnitude of how our sinful actions affect others, check out *Joshua 7:1-26*. God is so serious about this, I pray that we will all take Him seriously and think before we act.

~Thoughts~

The Long Arm of Disobedience & Deception

The Fall of Man: Genesis 3:1-13

Now the serpent was more crafty than any of the wild animals the lord god had made. He said to the woman, "did god really say, 'you must not eat from any tree in the garden'?"[2] the woman said to the serpent, "we may eat fruit from the trees in the garden, [3] but god did say, 'you must not eat fruit from the tree that is in the middle of the garden, and you must not touch it, or you will die.'"[4] "you will not surely die," the serpent said to the woman. [5] "for god knows that when you eat of it, your eyes will be opened, and you will be like god, knowing good and evil."[6] when the woman saw that the fruit of the tree was good for food and pleasing to the eye, and also desirable for gaining wisdom, she took some and ate it. She also gave some to her husband, who was with her, and he ate it. [7] then the eyes of both of them were opened, and they realized they were naked; so they sewed fig leaves together and made coverings for themselves. [8] then the man and his wife heard the sound of the lord god as he was walking in the garden in the cool of the day, and they hid from the lord god among the trees of the garden. [9] but the lord god called to the man, "where are you?"[10] he answered, "I heard you in the garden, and I was afraid because I was naked; so I hid."[11] and he said, "who told you that you were naked? Have you eaten from the tree that I commanded you not to eat from?"[12] the man said, "the woman you put here with me—she gave me some fruit from the tree, and I ate it."[13] then the lord god said to the woman, "what is this you have done?" The woman said, "the serpent deceived me, and I ate."

After studying this for my quiet time one morning, I sat and thought and wondered what would have happened if Adam had stopped Eve from eating the fruit, and stood for what was right and not eaten the fruit and obeyed God? After all, it's not like he didn't know what was going on because, in verse 6, it says that Adam was with Eve. God told Adam not to eat from the tree before Eve was ever created, so it's not like Adam didn't know.

Nevertheless, the fall happened. But why did the fall happen? Why are we all still paying for it to this day? It's because of disobedience and deceit. The enemy deceived, which he is doing now, very well may I add, because that's his native tongue; lies. Eve was deceived, she said it herself in verse 13. But isn't that what happens when we say that we're not going to do something, but then we start hearing this little voice of compromise, of doubt in our heads. We make the mistake of thinking we can handle temptation on our own and we don't look for or accept God's way out of tempting situations *(1 Corinthians 10:12-13)*. So, we give in to the lies, and we end up disobeying God. Then as if this wasn't bad enough, we try to cover up our disobedience or hide it from God as if He doesn't already know! What's even worse is that we run away from God because of our shame and self-condemnation instead of running to Him for forgiveness. *(Romans 8:1-2)*

God tells us in many ways throughout the Bible not to have sex before marriage, but we do it anyway. Granted, some people aren't taught God's ways or aren't taught to not have sex before marriage, I wasn't taught that. But those of us who know the truth and still do it anyway, well that's a different story. Disobedience leads to shame and guilt and loss of freedom in so many ways. When we give in to the temptation of having sex before marriage, we think that it's just sex, just for the moment, but disobedience stretches far and wide. We think our decision to have sex is all about us and our wants not realizing that it affects much more than just our little wants. In Genesis 2:25 it says that "the man and his wife were both naked, and they felt no shame." This is how God created us to be, naked before Him and to never feel shame. But disobedience brings about shame. Shame defined IS THE PAINFUL FEELING ARISING FROM THE CONSCIOUSNESS OF SOMETHING DISHONORABLE, IMPROPER, RIDICULOUS, ETC., DONE BY ONESELF OR ANOTHER. Shame is painful, and God never wanted this for us.

The decision to have sex before you're married stretches into your marriage. I believe this contributes to the high divorce rate; shame. Sex in marriage is soul-baring and intimate. It's the freedom to have sex with the one that God has blessed you to be with for the rest of your life. When you say, "I do" you have God's blessing to have sex. You can't be shameful in a marriage and expect it to thrive. You will have issues, I know because it happened to me in my marriage. In the beginning, I was ashamed to be free sexually with my husband because of the things I'd done in the past. Disobedience leads to loss of freedom. I was married to the finest man in the world and had the freedom, God's permission, and blessing to enjoy sex, and yet I felt shame and imprisoned. Sex before marriage ties your soul to the person you have sex with. If you have sex with multiple people before you're married and then you finally get married and haven't broken the soul ties, then guess, what? It all comes with you to your marriage. Don't we often think of our husbands as our soul mates? Soul ties can only be broken by the blood of Christ. If not broken, they can destroy your life. Soul ties are from the enemy, and his ultimate goal is to steal from us, kill us and destroy us. Total opposite of what God wants for us. As I've said before, what you do now affects your marriage. Marriage is not a magic wand! It doesn't make your issues just go away. If anything, marriage is the great magnifier!

A FEW CONSEQUENCES OF DISOBEDIENCE:

1. Brings about shame
2. Loss of freedom to enjoy what God has given us. (Genesis 3:7)
3. Doesn't just affect us but those around us
4. Cause us to lose God's best for us. (Marrying wrong person, children out-of-wedlock, etc.)
5. Leads to lifelong painful situations (STD's, AIDS, baby mama/baby daddy drama)

You don't have to have sex with someone to find out if they are a good match for you. That's a horrible way to go about this! Trust me, let God bring you to your husband *(Genesis 2:22)*. The last thing you want is to have your vision clouded by lust, and you end up missing out on what God has for you. Take this time to focus on you, becoming the wife you want to be now and praying for your future husband. He needs it!

~Thoughts~

What I Wish I'd Known about Sex before I Got Married

1 Corinthians 7:3-5
³ The husband should fulfill his marital duty to his wife, and likewise the wife to her husband. ⁴ The wife does not have authority over her own body but yields it to her husband. In the same way, the husband does not have authority over his own body but yields it to his wife. ⁵ Do not deprive each other except perhaps by mutual consent and for a time, so that you may devote yourselves to prayer. Then come together again so that Satan will not tempt you because of your lack of self-control.

What I wish I'd known about sex before I got married is how powerful it is! When my husband and I first got married, we knew nothing about marriage. At our old church, some of the members we'd gotten to know found out that we weren't married and began telling us that it's wrong to "shack up" or live together before marriage and that if we were going to continue to live together then we needed to consider getting married or one of us find somewhere else to live. So, we prayed about it and asked God if it was His will for us to marry, that He would make a way because we were still broke college students and had no help from family. It was just us. So, we met with our pastor, who told us "if you're having sex, stop until you get married". He found out we were living together, said we needed to marry soon, and that was it! No teaching on the roles of husband and wife, no teaching on sex, money, nothing! Anyway, a few months later, we were married, and all was well…for a while. See, once you say, "I do" you kind of tick off the enemy and you enter a whole new warfare. In this warfare, especially for us being ignorant about marriage, Satan had the upper hand it seemed, because we knew nothing. He used it to his advantage. Fast forward a few years and add in a child and all hell breaks loose! Why do I say this? Because this is where you really learn who you are, who your husband is, and you get familiar with your body and feelings toward sex. After you have a child, everything changes especially your body, and everything doesn't bounce back, especially your desire for sex. It takes a while. The first year can be crazy! Nursing, no sleep, and a husband whose body hasn't been altered, and he still wants and needs sex. I remember being angry, no furious, with him for even daring to mention sex! Did he not know how tired I was and that if one more person touches my breast, I will scream?! So, for a while, our marriage kind of tanked, rose, ebbed, exploded. I didn't know or understand my husband's need for sex and how his needs differed from mine. Satan doesn't mind using one of the most beautiful events against your marriage, the birth of a child. So, how is sex powerful? Sex is like super glue in marriage. An active sex life warrants closeness to your spouse and to God. It's an important foundation for marriage. Sex, with the help of God, of course, helps to create this impenetrable force, this bond, between you and your husband. The more you satisfy each other sexually, the happier you are in your marriage and outside of your marriage. It won't solve all your problems, but it creates a bond for the two of you that helps you to fight together for your marriage, instead of fighting each other and against each other. The power of sex is to men like spinach was to Popeye, it gives them super strength, it boosts their ego, strengthens them to take on the world, gives them security, helps to protect them from temptation. It provides the same things for you as a wife. This powerful act can only come from the wife and guess who knows this as well? Satan. There will be times when you will have a headache, tummy ache, bubble guts, work to finish, issues with the kids, craziness at work; anything to make you not want to have sex with your husband. There will come a time, many times, when the absolute last thing on your mind is sex! Now, here comes the hard part. According to 1 Corinthians 3-5, you are not supposed to say no…I remember having a conversation with an older lady a long time ago about sex and marriage, and I asked her what you are supposed to do when he wants to and you don't, and she said: "lay there until it's over!" LOL! I will never forget that! Let me tell you, please don't try this! Sex was created by God as a wedding gift! You can't just lie there and wait for it to be over! God didn't create something so wonderfully pleasurable for us to just lie there! I've learned that sex requires us to die to ourselves; it deals with the selfishness in our hearts. It's not always about how we feel or what we want. DO NOT BE FOOLED BY WHAT YOU SEE ON TV! Those hot and heavy scenes are scripted. Not to say that there will not be moments like that, don't get me wrong, I'm just saying that sex will not always be hot, heavy, clothes everywhere…that way! Now, I've talked to a few wives who practice "withholding". I'm guilty of that as well. There are several reasons that women withhold. Anger, frustration, lack of security in the marriage, lack of affection, lack of sex drive, or they're just plum tired! I've heard suggestion after suggestion on how to deal with this, but the bottom line is you need to find ways to help to get you in the mood unless you and hubby have decided that ok, not tonight or not now. But it must be consensual, if not, be prepared to feel the conviction. Turning your hubby down for sex is a rejection for them. In their eyes, you've rejected them! I was floored the first time I heard that! I'm thinking, I just want to sleep and while I'm sleeping he thinks that he's been rejected by his wife. Just going with the flow isn't always easy for women. For us, sex begins at the beginning of the day and in our minds. There should be communication and affection throughout the day. Not to mention, it's darn near impossible to relax and enjoy sex when you still have your to-do list running through your mind, or you haven't had a moment to yourself to breathe. You and your hubby must understand each other's personalities and bodies and go from there. As women, you have the God-given right to enjoy uninhibited sex with your husband. Withholding hurts you just as much as it does your husband. Sex improves your mood, appearance and increases the love you feel for your hubby. Sex within marriage is beautiful! It's incomparable to any other act. It imitates the relationship that God wants to have with us, the intimacy he wants to have with us. Its power is not to be taken lightly or abused. It's to be respected and cherished just as the husband and wife should respect and cherish each other. The world has it all wrong.

~Thoughts~

So, What Are You Bringing to Your Marriage?

Picture your perfect man; he is the finest man you have EVER seen, he smells so good all the time, he treats you with respect and can cook! He asks you to marry him, you have a beautiful wedding, then it's HONEYMOON time and then… you freeze up and can't seem to relax, let go, and enjoy sex with your new husband (insert laugh from the enemy)! You start to freak out, and wonder "what in the world is going on?" Before you got married, you couldn't keep your hands off each other! You make it through the honeymoon, and you begin your new married life together (insert the sunshine, flowers blooming, and birds chirping here!) You get used to being married, and sex becomes a non –issue, or so you think, but sometimes you don't want to have sex, he wants to ALL THE TIME! What's going on you start to think? More time goes by, and you get the "baby bug" and then somehow you want sex all the time, and your hubby thinks it's great! Then the precious bundle of joy comes along, and you realize OMG what have I gotten myself into because you now feel that there are several hundred other things on your to-do list…including sex with your hubby. By this time hubby is tired of playing second fiddle, but you just can't deal with his "selfishness" right now, and he should understand because after all, you're the one who carried this child, right? Doesn't he know that everything doesn't go back to the way it was after you have a baby, including your sex drive (not immediately, anyway)? So, you're married a few more years, and you have other spats, and you grow up together in marriage, and you find out things about each other that you don't like and you wonder again "what have I gotten myself into?" As a woman, our first inclination to hurt the man in our lives and to cut off "the goods". No sex for you mister! Not knowing at the time that's exactly what the enemy wants.

Sex is powerful! It has the power to build and strengthen your marriage and the lack of it in marriage has the power to tear it down. God created sex to represent the oneness that is marriage. Think about it, when you spend time with God, praying and talking to Him every day throughout your day and reading His word, it strengthens and deepens your relationship with Him. Same thing with sex and your spouse, it deepens and strengthens your marriage.

Now, say you've had sex with each other before you got married. It was the best sex ever! You were open to various positions, different places, times it didn't matter! What headache? I have to get up early for work but who cares, right?! When you have sex outside of God's will, it makes the enemy happy! The forbidden tastes so sweet, doesn't it? But once you get married, Satan can and will wage war against your marriage and guess what, he doesn't play fair, HE WILL USE YOUR PAST SEXUAL EXPERIENCES! Satan hates marriage. Why? Because it is blessed by God! You have entered a covenant with the Most High! God has blessed your union and what God has joined together let not man separate! You have officially ticked the enemy off. Satan does everything he can to get you to have sex before marriage and everything he can do to get you to not have sex when you get married because he knows how powerful sex is. He knows that sex is a wedding gift from God and it is good, and the enemy hates anything that is good and from our Father.

I have experienced most of these things in my marriage, and I have spoken to many other married women, some who've been married much longer than I have, who go through this as well, but sadly, they haven't dealt with their past sexual experiences or don't know the power of sex in marriage, and the enemy is having a good time destroying their marriages. Marriage is beautiful, but it is challenging work! It is by far the hardest quest ever for me sometimes. Why is marriage so hard, you ask? Because it requires you let go of you and serve your partner. You become a servant, and it's not always easy. Some days it's just beautiful, and other days I want to run for the hills! Ok, so what's my point? My point is, God has a purpose for sex and when you abuse it, there are consequences, and just because you get married, it doesn't make all the baggage go away. Everything you do now will have some kind of effect on your marriage. As I always say, what you do now, matters. The only way to deal with it is to not have sex before marriage, and if you have, like I did, then you better have God, because you're going to need Him! Marriage is not for the faint at heart, and neither is sex. It is very powerful! Sex before marriage opens you up to stuff you will wish you'd never had to deal with. You create soul ties with every person you've ever had sex with, and if you don't give that stuff over to Jesus, it's coming to your wedding, your marriage, and it's staying there! You and your future hubby must talk about your sexual history, deal with it before you say, "I do" because hiding it only gives the enemy ammunition against your marriage. He will cause you to remember stuff that you thought you'd forgotten about. He will cause you to compare your hubby to others in your past; oh, he doesn't fight fair at all! Go to premarital counselling or if you're not getting married anytime soon, still go deal with it, get rid of it before you get married. You will be so glad that you did!

~Thoughts~

About the Author

Shannon Taylor is a wife, mom, author and teacher whose great call is to teach God's daughters His truth about sex and purity. This call gave birth to her ministry Savin' it for Hubby. Savin' it for Hubby has opened new doors to allow her to bring truth to women from all walks of life.

Her ultimate goal is to lead women to the lover of their souls, Jesus Christ, and to teach them to depend on Him for their every need; whether it's mental, spiritual and/or physical.

Shannon resides in Suwanee, Georgia with her husband Richard and their three children Maya, Ava and Caleb.

To contact Savin' it for Hubby or to invite Shannon to speak, please go to http://www.savinitforhubby.wordpress.com or via email at savinitforhubby@gmail.com

Made in the USA
San Bernardino, CA
04 August 2018